The Best
of Bad
Faulkner

A HARVEST/HBJ ORIGINAL
HARCOURT
BRACE
JOVANOVICH

San Diego   New York   London

The Best of Bad Faulkner

CHOICE ENTRIES FROM THE
FAUX FAULKNER COMPETITION
plus Peter DeVries, Shirley Jackson,
Kenneth Tynan, Derek Willey, and
Ernest V. Trueblood (William Faulkner)

•

Edited and with a Preface by
DEAN FAULKNER WELLS

HBJ

Copyright © 1991 by Yoknapatawpha Press and
American Way Magazine

THE BEST OF BAD is a trademark of Harcourt Brace Jovanovich, Inc.

Library of Congress Cataloging-in-Publication Data
The Best of bad Faulkner : choice entries from the Yoknapatawpha Press
and American Way magazine Faulkner write-alike competition/edited
and with an introduction by Dean Faulkner Wells.—1st ed.
p.   cm.
ISBN 0-15-611850-5
1. Faulkner, William, 1897–1962—Parodies, imitations, etc.
2. Literature—Competitions—United States.   1. Wells, Dean
Faulkner.
PS3511.A86Z6283   1991
813'.52—dc20   91-22521

Printed in the United States of America

First edition
A B C D E

Permissions acknowledgments appear
on page 151, which constitutes a continuation
of the copyright page.

CONTENTS

CONTENTS

CONTENTS

CONTENTS

CONTENTS

CONTENTS

PREFACE

This was the bait:

> The flags waved in the inexorable dust of the somnolent hamlet as the avaricious old avatar sought sanctuary from the sound and the fury of mosquitoes swarming about the epicene body of his affable and profoundly unabashed comrade prone across the pagan catafalque as he lay dying.

Bad Faulkner was everywhere, like no-see-ums on a beach in July, but the Faulkner bug didn't bite anyone until *American Way* magazine teamed up with Yoknapatawpha Press and its *Faulkner Newsletter* and the University of Mississippi's Center for the Study of Southern Culture to create a "Faux Faulkner" Contest—and then the would-be Faulkners came pouring in from three continents like bonsai Bundrens waving their sheets of misbegotten prose and shouting that *theirs* was the best bad Faulkner in the world.

The idea for the contest came in the wake of the late, lamented Imitation Hemingway Competition sponsored by Harry's Bar and American Grill. For years we had enjoyed reading those fine, clean, big-game trophies, and it seemed inevitable that "Pappy" would follow "Papa" (should it have been the other way around?), that a *Best of Bad Faulkner* collection would evolve willy-nilly—and here it is.

The rules governing the "Faux Faulkner" Contest were beguilingly simple: Imitate the master's unmistakable style, themes, characters, or plot in a short-short story of up to 500 words in length and mail it to the *Faulkner Newsletter* (P.O. Box 248, Oxford, MS 38655) by the February 1 deadline. The winning contestant (Saul Rosenberg, 1990; Gregory Sendi, 1991) and a companion would be flown to Memphis, compliments of American Airlines, and thence fetched to Oxford (not by limo nor even by Caddy but safely), where the prize-winning entry would be announced during the University of Mississippi's Faulkner Conference in August.

As one contestant wrote, "This contest may not fly me to some sunken Italian city to have an exotic meal in a fancy world-famous bar and grill but it's the closest I'll ever get to [William Faulkner] and I can't resist taking a chance on it even if it *is* in Mississippi in the dead of summer. (The sentence went on for sixty pages, and that was only his cover letter.)

And they must have liked it, all the faux Faulkners panting in the closets of their imaginations waiting to release their Benjies and Benbows, Ikes and Ikkemotubbes, because the entries poured in from some 48 states, including Alaska and Hawaii, and U.S. territories, Puerto Rico and Iraq (just kidding), and from would-be Faulkners living in the south of France, Wales, Australia, Japan, Yugoslavia—and Mississippi, don't leave her out!

Who *are* these faux Faulkners? Well, they are college and high-school English teachers and their students, housewives and accountants, advertising executives and TV broadcasters, long-distance truckers, lighthouse keepers, stargazers—and a few "ringers," professional writers whose names cannot be revealed to protect their reputations, considering that they did not win. In 1990, 650 contestants battered us into submission with such titles as "Inclusion in the Rust," "As I Lay Dieting," "Abstinence, Abstinence!" and "The Round and the Furry." And 750 faux Faulkners had not had enough, returning to bedevil America in 1991. We won't even try to guess what's going to happen in 1992.

Alas, everybody could not win, though *The Best of Bad Faulkner* helps alleviate that unfortunate condition by releasing a broad selection of best/bad Faulkners into the world. Many wrote that entering the contest was a prize in itself because it rekindled an interest in reading Faulkner's works (take note, Random House) and served as a reminder of (1) our debt to Faulkner, (2) our debt to Flem Snopes, and (3) how damned hard it is to imitate Faulkner. As testimony to this last point, the "Smokehouse" section of this collection features some imitations that previously had found their way into print, including "Afternoon of a Cow," in which the master imitated himself.

So aspiring Faulkners obviously have had a good time writing, and we have had a whale of a good time reading. Our judges for the first two contests—George Plimpton, William Styron, Barry Hannah, Jack Daniels, and Willie Morris—worked into the wee hours to come up with a winner, which was no easy task. ("Was that stream of consciousness or the jet stream?" And he: "*Whew!* I'm finished, now." And he: "I dont hate 'em, I dont, I dont. . . .")

In his book *Faulkner's Mississippi*, Willie Morris tells how Walker Percy, as a freshman at Chapel Hill, was required to write a placement theme. Already a devoted fan of William Faulkner, young Percy wrote a paragraph without punctuation and wound up in the "slowest" section of freshman English.

"All I wanted to do," Percy lamented years later, "was write like Faulkner."

—DFW
Oxford, Mississippi

Pounded
in Fury

••●••

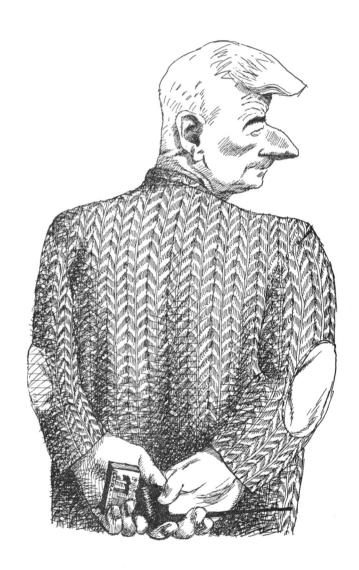

DOOMED

• • • • • *I*f he had been born with a talent for brevity or even the ability to construct a simple cohesive sentence, he might now be turning his attention to a different contest, that would take him, if he won, to a good bar, an honest bar in an Italian city, that even as a boy he dreamed of seeing, where he could drink for free with other Americans and feel good, but that was not to be so, for like all men who had grown up in this part of the country where time was measured not in hours but in the length of a planting season his words flowed like a tangle of Spanish moss dragged through the swamp grass, dooming him or perhaps (as the Preacher Bailey would say) preparing him for this other competition, that would ask him to call upon all his pedantic talents and probably those of long departed family as well to secure a measure of fame and also those two free tickets that the airline company was offering, that he knew was bound to attract anyone who possessed either a fountain pen or a dream to be rid of hot sticky sweet lands, into trying their hand and perhaps very soul while hoping, no matter how small or how slim the odds might be that they would be the one chosen and that their words (for at least one issue) would grace the pages of an "in-flight magazine" and in doing so would soar above the clouds and be carried out across the skies in every direction like the white cranes or the wild geese that he had watched while still a boy as he sat on the clay banks of the river dreaming that his words too might one day be read.

—*Jeff Sanders*

As I Lay Dieting

· · · · · *L*izzie
September 1, 1990
   then I seed her eatin hog meat, it was pig killin time, the swine of Euboeleus, she piled her plate full and red eye gravy on it like the vertiginous overflow of a bayou in spring on which a skiff, like a thrombosis floating on an artery blocked by gelatinous fatty primally controversial cholesterol, obstructs the passage out; and
I says, rosie beatrice
she quaffed the greasy elixir
I said, Rosie Bea, elevating my sisterly affection to upper case, and truncating her symbolic name,
stop stop stop
because its killing you, aye Godfrey, its killing you
Look at the clock *the minutes are calories* she answers no she answered Mind yo' own beeswax you are the sow not I.

Porah
September 1, 1989
   We have come a right fur piece to this funeral. I recollect Rosie Bea saying, once when she and Lizzie and I were no more than knee-high, I recollect it right well, she said, *After*

a certain age you got to choose either a pulchritudinous face or a pulchritudinous fanny. It was a delicately perfumed spring evening, the scent of lilacs permeated Mossrot, where Mama and Daddy and those servants we endured had all come some years before in a white covered wagon pulled by maculated horses. *Now*, Rosie Bea said, *Ive made my choice pass me some more pork chops.* Now Rosie Beatrice, refusing to enumerate her calories, has passed.

Beatrice Rose
September 11, 1911

My God it was only pork. How was I to know that my two sisters *they are both bitches I will not even use Freudian symbolism to describe them* would go on for eighty years about it, reversing my name in the bargain? Look at Lizzie over yonder, earth-heavy and violet orbed, thinking she has come to Mossrot for my funeral when indeed I am not dead but merely at a diet center which she, deaf as Tiresias was blind, misheard as "died a sinner." And Porah sensationalizing as usual; what I said that day was I am a pork chop survivor, I have joined a support group. We members of the human race have a soul, a spirit capable of sacrifice until the cows come home; I decline pork, I said, I will have tofu! I will! I decline it, I will have it, tofu, I choose tofu!

—Sam Staggs

THE WELL

. . . . . *H*e sat with his sister at the hill's base, looking up at the mound of earth relentless, the eminence of land unaccountable, the big pile of dirt: it seemed to grow higher in his eyes with each day, the mouth of the well it held deep in its bowels ever more distant. Not that he dreaded the walk up, nor the smell of her hair in the morning sun, the touching of their hands briefly, shyly, as they both reached for the crank to bring up the well bucket that always rose too soon and much too quickly. He dreaded what came after, the part of the journey that shook him to the core every time he fetched the pail of water: the descent, the dust slipping out from under the smooth soles of his worn boots, his heels giving in to unbroken gravity.

"Damn, Jack, are you just goin to stand there lookin up at it?" she said, smashing his ubiquitous veil of nostalgic morbidity and stomping on his foot as well. He reached down to rub his foot and pick up the bucket that lay there, taking it with a hand still callused from gripping the rungs of his mother's casket and dragging it across the field during the casket races at the big Obieonekenobie County annual picnic last summer. The memory of his fourth-place finish in that event filled him with further dolor.

"I'm coming, Jill," he said and followed her up the path, the path that every Sartoris before him had scaled, dating back to the very first Sartorises and even further, to the primordial Sartorisaurus and its scaly ill-fated broods of Sartorisauruses. His grandfather, the sartorial Cyrus Sartoris, a Taurus, had followed this very trail, spitting and swearing as he mounted each dusty turn, screaming in fear as he descended it. He had never been the same after that last fall, just sat in the parlor and claimed he was playing chess-by-mail with Stonewall Jackson until the day came when he went to reach for the bucket and instead kicked it through the window above the armory and fell like a bag of heavy shot as the chickens flew through the window and pecked at their broken reflections in his shattered reading glasses and the rains came and the floods started and . . .

"Jack, will you stop having flashbacks and hurry up with the bucket?" She had already made the top of the hill and was drawing water from the well. The bucket, the bucket, he had never wanted the damn bucket, but every Sartoris male had held the weight of it. He took it to her, set it down, watched as she filled it.

"Well, that's that," she said, handing him back the bucket. He felt the sudden heft of its plenitude. "Go on, then. Mother is waiting for the water to start breakfast."

"Mother's dead."

"Well, maybe, but she still likes her Cream of Wheat."

Jack faced down the hill. "How about you go first?" he said, but it was too late: the bucket's weight drew him down the precipitous decline, pulling him back-first down the hill. As he left his feet and felt his body topple end over end, he felt the relief of giving way to a larger force, although this feeling was combined with irritation at hearing Jill's convulsive laughter as he picked up speed, irritation that gave way to empathy as her spastic mirth caused her to lose her balance and follow him in quick violent descent down the hill. After them both came the bucket, now void of its watery weight, falling at a relaxed pace, banging from rock to rock in a symphony for no man.

—*Jay Martel*

I Lost My Place

• • • • • *F*ar back, before reading became remembering and remembering in its turn understanding; far back in the ever-dwindling stoic implacable yet not hurried or even fleet progression (outspilled from the lush fecund and eternally untamable copiousness of rhapsodic writerly excess) of undifferentiated inscrutable and at times nonsensical words, marching obliviously onward in perpetuity with endless imperious majesty and cruelty, compounded but immiscible of the ascension glory and assassination endlessly repeated of word supplanting word begetting word without respite quiescence or reprieve, no lacuna of ineluctable succession of generation upon generation; before even resentment of moiling syntax became repudiation: and repudiate I did, as we all do, perennially recanting the assertion of our pasts as much as our words; but that was not the point, as several others were not, including: the unquenchable gnawing eagerness or avidity perennially unrequited but indomitable nonetheless to find lying hidden in plain sight but unseen or maybe just condoned in this squandered ruin of a once invitatory text, making expressions long bereft of gentility and pretense of import, the facade of the dilapidated but once pristine edifice of thought, pure in its primal verity but now adulterated yet retaining the trace of its former semblance; besides the unnamed but recognizable substance and meat or both of meaning the grim final but comfortable from familiarity (which breeds many things other than contempt, whose true issue is itself) swift irrevocable peremptory stolid falling breath-giving and grammatically sensible appearance of a period: but this is not the point: antedating even the era when the first jot or conception of the progenitors of this began sus-piring in the humid circumambience of thought (penumbral auguries of, and redolent of, this dark that wraps in tene-brous folds once aimed to exfoliate but now suffocating), the precursor of all that came before this timeworn heritage of syllables—even before all else had chanced or designed to occur, I lost my place.

—*Michael Houdeshell*

BATHOS

• • • • • *N*ow there is no sound in the room save the soft hum of the crowd and the reassuring tone of Pat's voice. Joe does not move or reply. He stares straight ahead and sees the wall; he sees the only obstacle between him and his fortune. He reads a jumble of confused letters as an infant reads a newspaper, his palms moistening, feeling the loud silence. But the silence is broken by his utterance, a single syllable, a fateful sound that he regrets uttering the moment that it irrevocably leaves his lips and fills the room. *It is over* he thinks *I have failed and it is over* The silence is further broken by the strident, raspy, grating buzz noise that confirms his thinking and abruptly drops him back into silence.

They had come to town months ago. And the town came to them: people of all histories flocked to the place of their stay, attracted like so many flies to the sticky sweetness of the glamour, the glitz, the perpetual notoriety that accompanied the visitors. All who were enveloped in the sweet syrup were thinking, 'Maybe I will be selected,' knowing *It will not be me, cannot be me* Joe too thought and knew as he heard of the arrival on the radio. But knowing never severs hoping: he joined the town and said, "I have only to gain," as if justifying his action by insisting that there was no other alternative. He would later commend himself on this faultless logic, but now he was hesitant and still uncertain. Then he heard himself answer the questions he was asked, but he was so anxious that he was not an active member of the interview: he was hovering over the room, observing, sweating, wincing. Weeks later he was chosen.

The reprimanding buzz noise once again jolts his senses. And he realizes what has happened as he glances to his side: he sees a man as nervous and as defeated by the buzz noise as himself, as if he is staring into a mirror. "Back to you, Joe . . . ," comes Pat's voice, reaching into Joe's chest and accelerating his heart with the false sweetness, the implication that something had to happen. A moment of silence passes, and Joe again makes an utterance; no grating noise follows it. His ears are instead bathed in a pleasant melodious note, and Vanna slithers across to reveal his fortune. He thinks, 'It is finally over,' thinking *I have won. I have done it, I have won*

—*Joshua Winn*

DID YOU EVER HAVE A SISTER?

• • • • • *D*id you ever have a sister? asked Lena
as they swished through the Grove. The savage light of the
August dusk shimmered against their shinyslick neon flesh
bicycle shorts as the two girlshewomen abandoned the wisteria womb fertile fragrance to stride down Sorority Row.
She the honeyblond perfect innocent the career virgin active
i the unspoken dark evilness the corrupted rushee she the
pristine Delta lineage the triple legacy sheen i the nouveau
Metarie car dealer the status grasping gleam she the new
convertible BMW i the shared '83 Cadillac *No No a brother*
Did you? *No* Because from now on mine and my sisters'
house will be your house and mine and my sisters' lives
your life And passing the parade of looming columns i saw
a temple of cash and jewels a sanctuary from my secret
suburban putrefaction a high tower of shelter from the black
burden of middle-class blood Oh thats right I know your
brother *Yes* He drives that Caddy *Yes A Caddy* Theres nothing quite like the love between a brother and a sister *No
no a brother* I just know youll love our brother fraternity
Yes In fact you can be a little sister *Yes* And as they turned
into the square the fireflies winking in silent conspiracy

twinkling her stickysweet periodic filth shame with honey-suckle innocence or rather the memory of it her pungent virginity stench swelling overripe in fragrant ruination with the odor of honeysuckle all mixed up until as the little belles paused in the window of Neilsons the Confederate soldier looking over the single shoulder of their bittersweet reflection framed in a dreamy timeless chiaroscuro she I just love your scent *Yes a brother* Is it Obsession *Yes* No its just my base my foundation And rounding the courthouse in golden undulation Lycra loins the seducer and the seduced one in abnegant transference as the yawning shadowblack orifice of night swallowed the final light *Did you ever have a sister* and she My my a body does get around.

—Elizabeth B. Boyd

AUGUST 27, 1945

•   •   •   •   •   *L*ooks like she's down a coupla quarts," Snopes said, peering at the dipstick. The blackened oil reached nearly to the full line.

"Then put 'em in," ordered the officer, turning to look again at the woman inside the office.

"What do you mean he isn't there anymore," Caddy said slowly.

"Sorry, ma'am, our record shows him dee-ceased las' year."

"And the body, what did you do with his body?"

"Patient without kin gets cremated."

Caddy lowered the telephone and moaned to herself, "Poor Benjy." Then she hung up.

Couldn't you have waited just one more year and I would have been back to get you out of there out of that hospital I couldn't get back before I didn't know how much you meant to me until the camp and then I couldn't.

Caddy stepped out of the darkened office into the searing sunlight. Reflexively her hand came up to shelter her eyes.

"He's gone," she said.

"I told you so. This town is a waste of time. Let's get rolling. We can still make New Orleans by tonight."

Caddy pushed aside the pint bottle as she got into the

front seat. The khaki-suited man gunned the engine, shooting out a spray of gravel.

You were what kept me alive I thought of you every day I'm sorry Benjy the one person in this world who needed me who accepted me as I was though you knew no better could never know any better I thought you loved me I thought you of all of them would wait for me.

The wind flapped her blouse as they drove. Even in August she wore a starched white long-sleeve blouse, sleeves long enough to cover the blue numbers tattooed on her forearm, sleeves hot enough on this Jefferson Day to be the first installment on the penance to which she had just unknowingly mortgaged herself.

Benjy your eyes were always looking at me I liked that I liked your attention but they were dull eyes staring without life I've seen many eyes like that now eyes with nothing your eyes only sparkled through reflected firelight.

I had to do it to get out of there to stay alive I had to do it.

Snopes watched the Packard disappear into the hazy mirage hovering over the asphalt. The upper girders of the trestle bridge formed a mouth that swallowed the fading vision whole.

Aint seen her in almost twenty years, Snopes thought, but she still holds herself like a Compson woman. He wondered if the old Packard would make the county line being driven that fast before the two extra quarts of oil damaged the engine. He didn't think meanly, just wondered, then Snopes went to get the tow truck ready.

—A. P. Boss

THE READER

• • • • • *K*nowing knows before remembering can ever have remembered that knowing was thinking about anything that remembering could have known.

The sentences of Yuckhuffapuffa County were deep and he had many to go before he could sleep and know he was literate, know that he had come face-to-face with Old Bill, alone, without Cliffs Notes, in the dark, mysterious, mute depth of the looming tome—seen him, known his power, felt the accumulated ages of wisdom and wordiness that he who could not be fathomed unless he allowed it by virtue of his pact with his own nature which had necessarily changed by accommodating to man, for man, though man knew it not and seemed to care not however much he lived and spoke and breathed the words bore.

And suddenly, emerged from a clearing of dialogue, there it was, over a page in length, exactly as Spam Feathers and Major Deegan and Christian Brothers and the Composts had said it would be. It was the largest sentence he had ever seen, white with clear traces of black and part French. He was so close to it now he could see a participial clause as long as a snake hanging from one of its branches. He read in awe as it swung its massive purport directly toward him and then veered, lumbered into a descriptive passage, its absolutes uncoiling darkly seemingly surreptitiously in peristaltic rhythms with plot references myriad proleptically plopping onto the leaves yellow-fringed and immemorial.

He read in a dense fog, trying to get his bearings, listening to the sonorous baying of verb and adjective as he followed the trail over the rough syntax with thorny clauses embedded in it to grate and trip an unwary man, expecting at any time to find a period in the litter of dark, lush prose strewn with semicolons and dashes while all around him the deep, chaptorial abyss yawned, suffocating him and he was reading reading reading, thinking never to find his way out as participles dangling from huge parentheses slapped him in the face and a dense tangle of verbiage caught at him, spinning him about, disorienting him, spinning him into an ever tighter cocoon of miscomprehension until, stumbling over leaf after leaf, gasping, thinking it would not end, could not end because the words were from the beginning while man was here only to use those words, to nurture and be nurtured by them, he saw a white space in the dark mass of characters and came, wheezing, agonizingly, and finally abruptly to the end and knew he had endured.

—Marshall Toman

DELTA FAULKNER

*T*hey came that year as they had come the year before and would come again the year after: the editors and publishers and critics good bad and indifferent but mostly indifferent and some just to say *Oh yes the Faulkner conference I made one* and even the representatives of an airline who had come to award a prize on the lawn of the stillupkept colonial mansion to that one who man woman or child could write as well as he could when he didnt and wise too not because it was easy (it wasnt) and not because it would do their airline any good (it wouldnt) but at least it was possible because heaven help anyone who thought he or she could write as well as he could when he did; the mansion upkept still though the very bones of its erstwhile owner (himself owner and proprietor too of that two thousand four hundred square miles of land more famous than any actual or apocryphal in the whole peopled continent) which had held together long enough to support the spirit that produced the work in what agony what sweat had long since returned to the annealing immemorial dust.

They came to talk. They had talked now for forty years and would talk forty more, and each year there would be a little less of the rich unbroken alluvial virgin ground: the new critics and there was plenty of room because it was just a trickle and the structuralists and there was still plenty left and the poststructuralists and it was a stream but that was all right because streams until at last it was a flood and all right still because when the new historicists (and who to know till then that the old historicists were old) came the deconstructionists had gone ahead clearing the ground before them and even this was all right because beneath it all lectures seminars symposia books papers whatever were the old bright words running strong illimitable and free; and the new ones not wiser or better but just younger and what they said not richer or truer but just flashier so that in all that echoing sound and iterant fury only the names had changed and over it all as if evolved by the old tales and telling out of the circumambient air there mused terrific somnolent and profound in the augmenting and defunctive twilight the figure of a man unimposing to the sight but to the mind a giant who had created out of the history of an old dead land and time rich in glamour and fatality and richer still in doom a fable that could never die.

—*Saul Rosenberg*

Old Jeb

• • • • • *H*e realized later that it had begun long before he had been born or was big enough to see and remember and tell afterward so that it would make any sense to anyone except maybe the vice president. It had begun insofar as the boy could discern when that first doomed creature made its first doomed attempt to slink out of the primordial sludge and into the vast indomitable wilderness and, once there, to discover within its heart the audacity, the courage and will to ask to be called a huntsman, a hunter, a courser, a stalker, a pursuer, or simply a good sport. It had already begun, he realized, on that day when the very first woman-weary band of such creatures had at last, in deliberate confederation against their ultimate evolution from men into a race of talking potatoes, slouched out of the town and into the big woods; had slouched into the big woods for a pristine and virginal breath of hushed and unflaggingly silent, pine-laden air, in blighted and desperate search of an opportunity to practice male bonding and to discover some excuse for ordering more than four hundred dollars' worth of stuff from L. L. Bean. The ineradicable truth was that man will endure, which cannot be said of American-made cars. And man will not merely endure: he will dress nattily when the occasion calls for it.

The bear, which was called Old Jeb, was old; so old in fact that he could remember when Carson was still funny. To prove his great old age Old Jeb stood up from the rotting log and stretched his front paws skyward to show the boy and the man the faded trace of a wound received at Chickamauga. The boy looked at the faint, ancient scar but said nothing. Col. De Sac slapped his knee, a loud thwack. "You 'spect us to quit huntin' you after all these years on account of some conjuration about a hole in the ozone?" he said.

Old Jeb sat down again on the rotting log. "Look," he said. "I think I can explain this a whole lot better—and you'll be in a whole lot better frame of mind to listen up—if we have another drink or two from that there bottle of your bourbon."

"Hell fire, you have had enough!" Col. De Sac said. "If shootin' cows is more sensible use of huntin' folks' ammunition, I would say you have had enough!"

"Cows are the cause of the hole in the ozone," Old Jeb said. "Cow winds are what put all that methane gas in the air. Methane gas is what is putting the hole in the ozone. It's a simple, scientific fact. Better for the environment to be shootin' cows than shootin' at me. I reckon we should be allies. Why, I can even lead you to some cows. But first, let's have that drink."

He is talking about shootin' cows, the boy told himself. *For nothing less than environmental protection. Now at long last folks can cite an excuse for shootin' cows other than it was an accident or sheer dumb stupidity. Yes, I see! I see! I see!*

"For God's sake, you call this bourbon?" Old Jeb said. He smiled and winked at the boy. "I've had better swill than this in Memphis cathouses!"

—*Robert F. James*

LITE IN AUGUST

• • • • • *L*ena thinks, 'I have come from Alabama with a banjo on my knee.' She thinks I *could have walked faster if it were in a case and I were carrying it, or if I played the harmonica.* Thinking: *why do I think in italics sometimes and sometimes in single quotation marks?*

Lena is walking to Georgia, to find the man who put her in the family way. She is also pregnant. What she does not realize is that the man has gone to *Soviet* Georgia, and the walk will be longer than she had hoped for.

"I am looking for a man named Burch," she tells a man who, in the most unbelievable coincidence ever recorded in southern fiction, is, in fact, Burch. He has had liposuction and let his hair grow out, so she does not recognize him.

"I dont know no one named Burch," he tells her. And to throw her further off the scent he adds, "In fact, I dont know no one named Church, or Lurch, or Snurch either for that matter, just in case you was thinkin' he might have changed his name, which is just the kind of thing a scoundrel like that might try." He is right pleased with his ruse till she says,

"How did you know he is a scoundrel?"

Burch stammers, "Er, well, you see, that is . . ." He grandiloquizes, "As per our discussion, be that as it may, we must prioritize, let's have lunch." He says, "Abba dee, abba dee, that's all folks," and pretends he has forgotten how to speak English.

"One more thing," she says, scrutinizing him closely, which is how she scrutinizes everyone. "Why is it you do not put an apostrophe in *dont?*"

"I am speakin' in dialect," he says, "and I must save up my apostrophes for my gerunds, from which I habitually drop the final *g.*"

"Burch used to drop his *g*s too," she sighs. "I was always finding them on the bathroom floor or wedged into the cushions of the Barcalounger." She sighs again and again, fogging Burch's glasses.

"You are hyperventilatin'," Burch informs her.

"That is because I have insufficient carbon dioxide to trigger my medulla oblongata."

Burch takes this as a cue and presses his lips to hers. She still does not recognize him, because he has had collagen injections like Barbara Hershey. He kisses her deep and long, like someone finishing a slush puppy.

She tears herself away. "My heart!" she cries.

"In conflict with itself?" Burch surmises.

"No, I have arteriosclerosis," she says, but such abstruse sarcasm is lost on Burch, a product of the rural South, who never even went to med school because he couldn't hack organic chem.

They stare at each other for what seems an eternity but is in fact only several weeks. Finally, Lena blinks.

"I win," Burch says softly.

"I had something in my eye," Lena says, softlier.

"Tough noogies," Burch mouths silently.

"Best two out of three?" Lena communicates via ESP.

But both know it is time to go. Lena's belly is as big as a zeppelin, and Burch must get on home to wait for the cable guy.

—Mark Silber

The Rest Is Silence

• • • • • *F*rom behind the fence, I can see them gathering before the jailhouse: the men and women and mules of Jefferson. Even a bear growls from somewhere in the crowd. Sheriff Hampton sits before the door, lazy and immutable.

"I reckon I know what y'all want," he says.

"You reckon right," Colonel Sartoris says.

The sheriff enters the jail and emerges with Gavin Stevens. In the glare of the torchlight, Gavin appears round and profound, like a balloon that does not know it is doomed to not-balloonness by the prick of an inescapable but fortuitous pin.

"You all think you can shut me up . . ." Gavin begins.

"Save it!" Popeye snaps. "Yer explainin' days are over."

The man sets aside his baked dog long enough to say, "Yao!"

The crowd moves Gavin to a nearby tree like a ripe plum borne on a sea of live ants. Gavin begins to shout, "Listen to me . . . ," but is cut short when Dilsey strikes him once in the stomach. I can see his jaw still working as Quentin fixes the rope around his neck, but I cannot hear the words.

Even after the rope starts to lift him from the ground, the jaws continue to work. He rises like a balloon tethered by a string, weightless, into the not-light and not-life of the evening sky, hanging there like a figure on a cross or a Phi Beta Kappa key dangling from a watch chain. Long after the body has shuddered into stillness, the lips continue their impotent travail, forming words to describe the outrage and despair of the obvious.

In the cricket-marred calm that ensues, Flem Snopes leans over and spits into the dust. "Guess this here is one story he aint gettin' the last word in."

"In the beginning was the Word. In the end was the Silence," Doc Hines says.

I hush.

—Geoffrey Bent

ABSTINENCE, ABSTINENCE!

. . . . . *B*ecause he knew. Had understood from the beginning, suspected anyway, from the speculative light in the old woman's eyes, faded watery dead eyes the light squirrel-gray of executioners' eyes, had guessed from the hooded, secret, avid glance and the tentative smile of the pressed lips, not the actual fact of her unthinkable purpose but the possibility at least, even, with sudden startled acknowledgment, the probability of it. And in that same half-knowledge, with that same dark instinct, the uneasy premonition of the dreamer, he had stolen the chicken bone—not because of a certainty, not because he knew, had planned, had organized his mind to what he must do with it, but merely because he sensed that it would be the instrument of their temporary safety and perhaps of rescue itself.

He stared through the bars at her, as she rummaged in the repellent artifacts of her craft on the far side of the cottage, and waited for his sister to awaken from her drugged sleep. For he presumed them both to be drugged constantly by the old woman, who plied them by the hour with her puddings and her bowls of syrup, drugged not by poppies (for there were no fantasies, no disengagement, no euphoric acceptance of whatever reality presented itself) but drugged through the sheer quantity of sweet, soft, warm food with which she had entranced them from the moment they had entered the cottage. They had eaten then, of course, had feasted, reveled, wallowed in food, it being two days since they had lost the trail in the forest to wander in sustained apocalyptic terror.

From the cage he watched her probing dimly at the great caldron on the hob—her sight was all but gone, as he had realized from the first ecstatic hour when she had heard them scratching tidbits from the very house itself and had hobbled out to greet them, exclaim over them, caress their cheeks and arms and even legs with a curiously purposeful stroke, the fingers insinuating, pressing, evaluating their substance beneath the ragged clothes—and removing laboriously the massive iron lid which she lugged with enormous effort across the flagstones, to drop awkwardly so that it crashed and spun like a gigantic coin, its blackened edges grating as it settled on the stone floor, gre . . . tel, gre-tel, gretelgretelgretel.

"Sister, wake up, she's coming," he whispered. "Here, take this chicken bone, and when she asks you to put out your finger, stick this out instead."

"Oh, Hansel, don't be silly," his sister said sleepily, but even as he handed it to her, he saw the awed, sickened comprehension aborning in her eyes.

—*Michael Kernan*

QUENTIN AND SHREVE
NARRATE THE RIVER-CROSSING
IN *As I Lay Dying*

• • • • • *S*o that long procession reached the river, eight of them with her in the box, and they never slowed or thought but plowed on through that water like Moses . . ."

"Wait," Quentin said.

" . . . through the Red Sea, the children following Anse like he was . . ."

"Wait, I tell you," Quentin said, though he still did not move or even raise his voice—that voice with its tense suffused restrained quality. "I am telling . . ."

Am I going to have to do this again? he thought; see this, hear this, smell this all again, and again live this sense-less (to me) ritual from which I am compelled to make sense by the ties of my geographical if not spiritual heritage; bound to witness forever the ritual of ghosts, carrying their own ghost in a box, and honoring the will of that ghost as if she were real and demanding in an audible voice a burial in Jefferson that she might witness herself?

"No," Shreve said. "You wait. Let me play for a while now. Now, Jewel. Jewel (that son of Addie's attempt at humanity with Whitfield, the servant and minister of his own desperate delusions), sitting there on that horse, the purchase of his nightly labors, seeing the turbulent waters with the eyes of his mother's still-living desire; bent, determined, obsessed with crossing that swollen river and never considering for a moment that crossing's cost to him, horse, or family. So he moved into the water, looking as if he alone were doing the moving, the horse being merely an instrument of his volition, volition which he administered to the horse through the incessant squeezing, prodding, speaking of his knees, tying the rope to his saddle horn and plowing the horse belly-deep onto the ford, the other end tied to the wagon as if by the sheer force of his will he could pull not only the wagon across the river, but Cash and Cash's doubting across too; not only Addie's coffin but Addie and her will, and not just across the river but all the way to Jefferson and clear into the not-yet-open but long-waiting and final ground."

"Wait!" Quentin said again. "For God's sake, wait. There was nothing heroic or transcendent about those people. They were ignorant, uneducated, inarticulate country people, acting out of stubbornness and dead expectation, their only knowledge being the unconscious recognition that they could escape the energy of Addie's will only by separating themselves from it with the soil of her Jefferson grave."

"Then maybe it was Addie herself who guided them across," Shreve said. "Yes, that's perfect; the ghost of Addie watching them all, only Vernon unseeing, watching herself in her own coffin and guiding them—Jewel, horse, Cash, wagon, Darl floundering in the current—across the swollen river to the completion of her own funeral rite . . ."

Quentin groaned: "Oh, for God's sake."

—*Mark O'Brien*

HE STARED WITH
A FIXED, UNMOVING GAZE

• • • • • *H*e stared with a fixed, unmoving gaze at the charred ruins of the Snopeburger Barn, remembering the sweet, slightly revolting smell of hot fat turning endlessly to vapor on a griddle, the mildly obscene costumes of the carhops, now unemployed, with the sewn patches of red cloth representing flames on their tight shorts front and back, another pair of flames over each breast, giving them the look of innocent demons as they roller-skated loads of hot food out to the waiting cars. He remembered, sitting and swinging on his front porch, when the Snopeburger Barn first was built, one of the many commercial ventures of County Commissioner Earl Snope, another way, some said, to hide the kickbacks skimmed from the building of the roads full so soon of potholes, the sewers cracking and disgorging their plagues of rats, the waterworks always in need of expensive repair. He knew better. Few of the current residents of the recently renamed Snope County, its population swollen by the nonunion General Motors transmission plant, would know or care about the grim joke lurking in the caricature of a barn decorated with painted flames and selling "Barn Burning Good" burgers, carefully located upwind of the ancestral home of Earl Snope's wife, fouling the air breathed by the brother she never saw. He remembered their last conversation, recalled precisely how she looked, tan in a way her female forebears never were from hours on foreign beaches, top-heavy from the silicone implants now worn by all the Snope women, wrists showing faint markings of bondage equipment, plagued by a recurring sniffle, starting as if in pain as she sat down, looking worn and diminished and a bit tired. He recalled her expression when she had finally explained to him why she persisted in such an unsuitable union, why she refused to return to this, the family homestead and live a life not filled with the coarseness and degradation that seemed to be flooding the world since the tragic outcome of The War Between the States; she had looked at him and said (he shuddered to recall it, even now), "Well, honey, Earl is a bit of a jerk, but I don't ever recall him being in a blue funk for a week because Hannibal defeated the Romans or whatever it was, and really, remembering the fun we had when we were younger, I do think I need to follow the teaching of the Good Book and put aside childish things, don't you?"

He remembered other things as well as he swung on his porch in the sweltering heat, remembered reading the *Iliad* in the original to that fourteen-year-old slut from the Snopeburger, how she would wiggle and squeeze him at the clash of armor, the birth of their idiot son, the towering rage that seized him when she ran off with the rock and roll band, the flames roaring up from the Snopeburger from the incendiary device he placed in the grease trap. There was some talk of a Tastee-Freeze locating on the ruins. Let them try. Just let them try. He was only a Snope by marriage, but just let them try.

—W. D. Cruse

Hedburn Didn't Sit
like a Statue

• • • • • *H*edburn didn't sit like a statue, with the mere absolute stoicism of that particular race of inanimates; no, his immobility, his meditative, calm, lack of movement, that stillness which seemed to include in its entity, for it was an entity, not just a description of his present mode of being but a constant and transparent, yet viscerally visible (yes, one could say visible, since the instinct sees more than those things that shadow) spirit, which enveloped and shared Hedburn's name, not sharing as a spouse or a brother, but as a nation shares with its inhabitants, that stillness which was beyond absolute, it was infinite. No one was more aware of this than Hedburn himself, who wore it like a priest wears his collar, as a nun wears her habit, as a knight wears his armor, for knight he was in a land of drawing Don Quixotes; who pondered this transparent uniform, this human-filled ghost, which meshed with the blue-black sky, that entered his field of vision through the crescent-shaped opening, while he sat motionless, resolute, and stern, his left hand poised, untrembling, on last winter's Montgomery Ward catalog.

—Jim Bailey

Aunt Dody's Funeral

*T*he coffin already sat on the mechanical contraption they used to lower it into the grave when the family got there. No point in going to the trouble of collecting a half dozen pallbearers who never knew her to come out in the cold on the day after Thanksgiving, who would be happy to do it if they had been asked because they knew the rest of the family, and their grandparents had known her before she moved away. From there it took little thought to decide that since there would be no church service there was no point in having a funeral car drive the family to the cemetery if there weren't going to be any pallbearers, and besides that it would make the cost of the funeral more appropriate to her style of frugality, though she had looked forward to everyone being at the funeral. If she had not waited so long to die, everyone would have to come to the funeral, but she outlived everyone she knew except the nieces, nephews, and distant cousins, and most of them were out of town for Thanksgiving so that it looked like they couldn't get a decent crowd in even the Presbyterian church, and it was a negligible size compared with the Baptist church. No point in having the funeral in the church if no one was coming, what with the added expense of taking the body to the church and then to the graveside which would also mean rounding up pallbearers and having two funeral cars which didn't really matter after all since the estate would pay the bill, but it seemed too sad to have a funeral in an empty church when everyone else in the family had all had big church funerals. So it wasn't really the money, but the last gesture of love and respect for the old lady who never had a chance for a church wedding, who looked forward at least to a church funeral. Rather than bring shame upon her with a service no one attended, they denied her the church funeral taking the reproach on themselves for a poor turnout, letting the whole town talk about how peculiar they were for having a graveside service with it threatening snow, providing the excuse for no one coming and thus the vindication for her by holding the service by the graveside with the wind whipping down the hill from the Confederate Monument where Sheriff Ligon stood with his granite back to us all while we huddled under the tent, and still there weren't enough of us to fill it up. She had devoted ninety years of living to dying so she could have a happy funeral where everyone would hear the gospel, but as I looked at the tiny band of nieces, nephews, and cousins shivering in the unyielding November cold, there wasn't a miserable lost sinner in the crowd. It didn't matter. I preached the gospel anyway for Aunt Dody.

—Harry L. Poe

The Warp and the Weft

• • • • • *H*e hoisted the ponderous material hermetically enveloping his slumbering frame and obtunded the insistent progeny of resplendent dawn that, like the phantasmagoric images of chimerical sleep, obtruded themselves on his somnolent sensibilities. He rose and gingerly traversed the dust covered floor, stepping slowly, the floor inveighing against his chilled feet, the pressures of consciousness already saddling his weary mind, stabbing relentlessly with their jagged spurs as if to wrest from him the tryrannical resolve which prompted him through his morning ritual. He pierced the sanctuary encasing the long velvety tubes, the quandary that loomed inexorably suddenly enshrouding him with disquietude, which neither facilitated decisiveness nor garroted resolution, but rather propelled him into a paralyzing abeyance, that, though staying the discomfort of decision, only prolonged the tormenting conundrum that immured him within the lining of his own heart.

He groped confusedly among the cornucopia of variegated garments, benefactors of the initiative of their possessor, who, insatiably inventive, had signed his ingenuity on these wan and disconsolate coalitions, adorning them with color borne from the iron rich soil and the blood of hapless verdure, yet, as he'd sat dyeing, he'd discerned the repercussions of his action, that, by advancing heterogeneity, fostered dilemma. The necessity of action became immediate, the wintry air caressing his sanguinary appendages, insidiously diluting complacent warmth with the pinch of encroaching numbness. He wrapped his gaze around the diverse plentitude, inviting distinction from the competing alliances in order to obviate the imminent endorsement of one creation over another, that, by virtue of exclusion, would vitiate existing parity. Each reached violently for his attention, blitzing him with brilliant hue and design, the sound and the fury of the incursion sheathing reason with irrationality, forcing him to disregard loyalties and exalt practicality. Unvanquished, he chose argyle.

—Eric A. Schade

Go Down, Goldilocks

• • • • • *S*he emerged, surfaced—obscurely juxtaposed against the unaxed woods and relinquished herself
to it: stood, seventy years before she could or would stand
defunctive of the old time, the old trees, the older people:
prefecund concupiscent and unfabricated. Emerged: to the
semicleared clearing and the unpainted clapboard house,
swamp-sunk and decayed, the door hanging by one corncob,
the sagging steps which she negotiated bought and amor-
tized as if by instinct, knowing what it would be like even
before she entered: the bear-rank room, the chairs then the
porridge: gelatinous cold indomitable and gaseous. Then
she was there before it, behind it, under it; not having moved
but simply there, somewhere, aware of what it would taste
like but doomed to taste anyhow and finally to eat in impotent vengeance and regret. The cold mass touched her
lips and tongue, then fell: bounced off the table, along the
tilted floor, and out the sagging doorway. Not having eaten
what she did not want or need, she searched the gloom for
the chairs, mute and eloquent evidence of ursine occupancy,
for the rest she did not want, could not accept nor resist:
one big, bigger than she had extrapolated or preconceived,

towering over her; the next just big, implacable presumptive and exacerbated; the last smaller: preoccupied and exfoleaceous. Sat, foreknowing the preordained inevitable event: it creaked, groaned, towered, crashed to earth like the doomed woods of her youth; not to the earth but to the porridge-slick floor from which she arose. Foreknowing too the beds she would find as she ascended and absolved the dimness of the stairway, of the ravished and virginal oblivion as she relinquished herself to it, and the bears: huge, rank and flatulent, looming over her as she held her nose and felt the first foreshadowing of verbosity and gastric repudiation.

"Ha. So you had to do it. In spite of Papa Bear's and your fourth cousin's coeval's descendants' warnings. And your knowledge of the accounts: your own story and legacy. You knew this was bear country and a bear house already, but you had to do it anyway. In the bear's own bed yet. I . . ."

"Yes. Vouchsafed and acknowledged, not against the repudiated porridge, but worthy of bequest by the dispossessed bears, presumptive of gnawing rapacity and grace. Dont you see? I reckon they foreknew I'd do it in spite of that; finally in atavistic anticipation of all regurgitation. Done."

She was out of the bed, hand to mouth, stumbling headlong down the newly rank stairway to the kitchen, sliding across the mucilaginous floor to the doorway and down the decayed steps, then moving soundlessly across the overgrown undergrowth, knowing without looking what she would see if she turned: the bears, juxtaposed in profound verbiage and humidity, behind the vacant gazing unglazed windows.

They endured. Barely.

—Ralph Schneider

SHOLY

•　•　•　•　•　*W*e got the whole slew nonetheless. I didn't know all of them, 'course, but I knew them all, like the way you kin hazard a guess on how a weasel's tenth generation's gonna act even if you never witness it. I couldn't git enough of that Gate: every one suspicious when they come in, furtive, askin Well then what's *he* doin' here? or this one there if we got rules, commandments? Lawyer said he would expect St. Peter to have the omniscience or horse sense to sequester them all to separate planets where He might stand a chance at some semblance of order, but that Bill had actually advised You might herd them if you plan on avoiding war or keeping Heaven and Hell in polarity. The Saint said Well, you made them; you said ain't nothing dead that ever was and you have been vindicated. You made them, He said, and Heaven ain't Heaven if it ain't Hell, too, partways at least. And heard Bill said Wait a minute, *You mean*— And the Saint said Just watch and Bill said he didn't believe there could be such a thing as an exculpatory spectator, said *You mean left to their own devices?*

Gavin figured that at least cleans up the notion of Paradisiacal ennui.

And me thinking Heaven help Him even before I come upon Flem at the Gate, said,

Hey, Flem. And he,

Hey, V. K. and looking at not me nor the Saint he asked it like the very words was the furthest thing from his mind, said he was jest tryin' to git a handle on what kind of tariff or toll St. Peter figured He was capable of extractin' at this game. And St. Peter with the expression of a man about to realize the rope he's been hauling in is a crocodile's necktie.

I saw Flem at the Gate often and me still able to believe that something cannot be and saw Bill shaking his head and was all there when I.O. waltzed in and gave two looks around and decided You kin take a horse to water or to Heaven but as the crow flies the cat is jest as eventual out-a the bag as sure as a miss is pert near good as a mile in St. Louie.

And Bill jest shaking his head, smiling a little this time.

So when Flem did quit visiting the Gate I am a Fool and figured he got tired of realizing you can't barter with a angel even if you do got something to swap, and I was there as if to assure me I am a Fool when Eck, within clear and naive earshot of Flem, wondered aloud if Peter might not sell a little land or if it was just laying around Eternity for the taking and I didn't look at Flem but I watched him while he arched one clean high spit, waited for the dust spark to subside and said Well

It ain't zactly His'n t' sell.

And I knew it would be just that, that right after he said it I was gonna know I knew it would be that all the time.

—V. K. Ratliff
(R. Mark Cassity)

The Old Colonel

• • • • • *A*nd so the old Colonel used them the only way he knew how, the spices eleven of them and the chickens themselves countless untold bucket- and barrelfuls, the woman his wife not even waiting any longer for the day when he would walk into their dustbrown dwelling with the fur piece—sewn with a label bearing a name she could not pronounce or even have read except with the deepset pebble eyes of her womanknowing—waiting even until the day twenty-seven years later when Ratliff would himself walk into the tiny well-lighted franchise in Jefferson ahead of a meager but unrelenting puff of dust and say "extry crispy" to the girl behind the register, not because it was what he wanted nor because it was not original recipe, but only because she had thought to ask him, thinking *I reckon a woman even a girl like she is is jest all asking and no knowing. I reckon a woman dont care one way or another whether a fellar has two wings and a breast or a drumstick and a thigh or whether his chicken is crispy or not jest so long as she can be asking fellars the same questions a hundred times a day or more.*

"D'you want coleslaw with that, V. K.?"

That he was a colonel Ratliff knew owing not to the fact he had seen him before (though he had seen him, years earlier, as a child, when the old Colonel lived in penury with his wife and a hundred thousand chickens, it seemed), nor owing to the white linen suit turned abject with chicken-filth, nor owing to a fact he (Ratliff) could not have known, that his (the Colonel's) old pioneer grandfather had taken his wife's family name because Saunders was more English than Poulet and that his odious antebellum father had changed it from Saunders to Sanders because it was more American, but owing to the remnants of a regimental gait the old Colonel, sworn as he had once been to the idea of his own perpetuity, could not yet know he was no longer able to preserve. Now under the sway of his command was neither regiment nor wife nor even the chickens, countless in number, and when Ratliff heard the woman, the wife, tell the old Colonel *You done brought me all the way to M'ssippi. A fur piece*, he did not yet even fail to remember how not to know that she would also say *Do something with them chickens* and again *a fur piece* and again *chicken* and then *of course, chicken* until it had taken root in the fertile soil of abjectness and longing that he could not yet even fail to know nor yet even long to forget was the blackbottom of what was not even yet not inside him anymore.

And Ratliff thinking, *I jest never reckoned the old Colonel would go this far on jest chicken, but I reckon a woman in her way can make a fellar do jest what she wants even if the fellar is a colonel, even if after everything all he has left to his own name is jest them eleven spices he puts in this here chicken even if alls a fellar can see left of him is jest them bones.*

—*Gregory Sendi*

THE BORE

• • • • • *T*he graduate returned to the red-moist region which had birthed him, a hundred miles square of woods unaxed vast and unreplicate, piny where it was not a mahogany-dark marsh or clay-pink, sliding river. He had an education and knew Proust and property values and set at once about his labor which he perceived as time-steeped and light-borne: development which became envelopment, bringing not mere Man but Appetite. Ribbed with honed skills both geometric and financial he swaggered, eyes scythe-sharp, and swift enough became himself a long legend of black-shacks knocked down and rifled of their tattered heritage, of rusted-out Sunday-outing pickups denied access to the ancient sandy ribbon-roads, of brambles and bobcat and even bear carried bodily away and devoured in dumpsters or dining rooms, of overalled hunters driven out, of condos slicing through moss-threaded boy-haunts of the graduate himself, of puny bird-lovers blown away by injunctions and writs—an eye-glazing legend of stultifying talk and Latin legal phrases which nonetheless carved a corridor of wreckage and wrath through which spread, not fast but with the ruthless momentum of monetary mass, the inexorable miasmic gray doom brought by the three-piece-suited graduate. Numbing was his novocaine presence, yet his lumbering inertia continued down to the final and most humiliating emblemishment. It squatted there on the river-bank, erected of pine paneling showing amber varnished knots, air-conditioned to ice cream chill, housing mutely the pastel cocktail hours ripe with chardonnay and forlornly bereft of Jim Beam—it was for those addled and aged enough to remember the old times, the ultimate horror: a country club packed full of lawyers. And worse.

—*Gregory Benford*

HIM

It was Ratmound telling this. That was what I thought, that was who Uncle Nilly said it was who was doing the telling to Uncle Villy who was doing the telling to Phlegm who was doing the telling to Varnish who did the telling to me who was doing the telling to Chips, but maybe it wasnt, not because Ratmound could not do the telling on his own but because not he, Ratmound, the sewing needle agent, could weave, spin, tell such a tale told to me alone, not he nor any one of them could tell the tale told to me alone because no one of them knew all they needed to know to tell the tale told, so all of them, he, Ratmound, the sewing needle agent, and Uncle Nilly and Uncle Villy, the twins, and Phlegm and Varnish had all created, added to, modified, and traduced the tale into what it became when I heard it, which is what I think happened, but I could be somehow wrong, mistaken, at fault, in error. So the tale, ad hoc dignus vindice nodus, I will tell you, ad hominem, coram non judice.

A latin phrase, he, Quentin, thought, thinking of Grandfather as the implacable and immutable and inviolable dust rose from the desk, disturbed by the aspirant invisible breath coming from his, Grandfather's, bed, rising into myriad motes of light which crept by the sash. Grandfather said I give you this phrase not because it will be of any use to you but because it is useless, so that you may learn that life is not all sarsaparilla and self-analysis, but that all endeavor and attempts and action are as futile and useless as trying to keep a sash free of dust. Then he died, and later he, Quentin, died, so that only his, Quentin's, ghost, and not his, Quentin's, body, remained and now was present in the office across from the town square (where a Confederate soldier facsimile stood in stone facing the omnivorous, never forgotten past, facing south where battles were fought and blood and dust rose into myriad motes of light), in the office where the lawyer, Gastric, and his, the lawyer's, Gastric's, nephew, C. Chips, talked.

"Do you ever dust this office?" Chips asked.

"Never," Gastric said.

"Well, you should," Chips said, moving his hand across the desk, disturbing the invisible, implacable, immutable, invincible, insensible, inviolable, involatile, immobile dust which rose into myriad motes of minuscule light, forming nearly noticeable nimbi in the office.

"There. That's better," Chips said. "What were you telling me of?"

"As I understand it from my sources, Banyard's sow just gave birth," the lawyer, Gastric, said.

"Oh," Chips said.

"Yes," Gastric said.

"You know," Chips, Gastric's nephew, said, "if you had a broom, you could knock down those cobwebs."

"I don't have a broom," Gastric said.

—Larry Thompson

GRANDFATHER SAID

• • • • • *G*randfather said:

We shall not speak of the time before the crossing (a time when the road was but a path, pounded, tramped through the brush, between the ancient, primeval trees, by the bare, callused—the soles cut, torn, by the sticks, the stones, the hard, black roots of the arboreal floor—feet of the Chickasaw; before the leather, rubber, rope soles of the white men trod the path—later bringing (the white men) the iron, steel shoes of horses; inexorably, ineluctably, grinding the brush into the dust, dirt, of the path, widening the path into a road—bringing axes, picks, shovels, plows, to chop, dig, turn the wilderness into farms, towns, cities (later the war would come, be brought; cannon, troops would follow it—the road—to their victories, their glories, their deaths) where the families of Compson, Sutpen, Sartoris, would raise great and small men and women) but of the time of Flem Snopes's prize hen's translation, migration, to the far side of that venerable roadway. Perhaps she (the hen) no longer wanted, desired, a life of pecking the dirt of Flem's yard (although everyone in Jefferson spoke of the abundance of worms in the fertile Snopes soil) or—and this was the opinion of the knowledgeable in the shadowed, mysterious ways of poultry—perhaps she was chased. When asked, he (Flem) would look up at sky, into the sun, rub his palms on his galluses, spit over his shoulder into the dust, and, slowly, chewing his plug as carefully as his thoughts—thoughts, ponderings, delvings into the nebulous reasonings of flightless fowl—he'd say:

"Aint ere a man give it as much thought as I," and here he would stop, looking off into the distance, repeating the phrase: 'aint ere a man,' then turn and look back at you, as if he (Flem) had forgotten you were there, continuing, "But I'm of the opinion she had a need to get to the other side." And as you left down that same road as the hen (and the Chickasaw queen; Issetibbeha, in her time) had crossed; Flem Snopes would not, seemingly, notice your absence from his side, instead he would stare at the inscrutable countenance of his hen, shake his head and mutter, "Aint ere a man."

—Terry Canaan

ABE'S SALOON! ABE'S SALOON!

*F*rom almost ten minutes past three o'clock until dusk of the long hot August afternoon (*as I lay dying in Yoknapatawpha General Hospital*) they sat in what old Miss Coldfurrow called Abe's Saloon because her father Abraham had called it that and because it served bourbon for fifty cents a shot and had a bar and tables and chairs and in the back, a room with a toilet that flushed and a sign on the door that read Men if you could read it. Opposite Quittin Cropson sat Miss Coldfurrow in widow's black eternal as death and black as the human soul in torment, a garment she had worn for forty-five years without thought of dry-cleaning it for what if she did and on that day He descended again and she wearing white or gray or blue or anything but black, what would happen then and who would have to suffer and die because of her woman's vanity?

"Tell me the fable again," Quittin said, " 'bout the Colonel and—"

"Tell it yourself," Miss Coldfurrow told him.

"Air you denyin' me the fable?"

"I air."

Outside, the light in August sucked your breath into a void no past could fill and no man yet born could name or deny. The old hound Moses jumped up on Quittin's lap. He had ticks big as fleas.

"Go down, Moses," Quittin said. "I got to git my boy at work."

Quittin left and started up the Plymouth and backed over Junior as he lay sleeping and drunk in the dust once, twice, the thump and ruckus under the tires a reminder of past debacles and deaths to come, and he opened the door and got out and fell to his knees and took his no-good no-account know-nothing son's head in his hands and wept.

"Where am I?" Quittin Junior asked, Goodyear tread across his forehead like some simpleminded grotesque tattoo.

"Abe's Saloon! Abe's Saloon!"

"Dont hate the car, Daddy. Hit was you drivin hit killed me."

"I dont hate the Plymouth, I dont," Quittin said. *I dont hate it!*

CHRONOLOGY

3:10 P.M. Quittin sits down with Miss Coldfurrow. The fable is denied him; bourbon is not.

7:30 P.M. Quittin gets up to fetch Quittin Junior at The Wild Palms Inn.

7:32 P.M. Quittin drives off to fetch Junior and instead drives over him, twice. Junior dies no more informed than when he was born.

GENEALOGY

QUITTIN CROPSON.

Grandson of Thomas Sootpan's first and only friend. Born, Jefferson, 1900. Attended Harvard Community College (HCC), 1920. Died, Jefferson, 1960. He did not endure.

ROSA COLDFURROW.

Daughter of Colonel and Goodly Coldfurrow. Died, Jefferson, 1950. Never dry-cleaned widow's garb. Never widowed.

QUITTIN CROPSON, JUNIOR.

Son of Quittin. Fetched by Quittin Senior in 1950 and subsequently run over by him, twice. Tire marks challenged the undertaker's art.

—John Ruemmler

ODE TO AMERICA BY GEORGE BUSH
AS RECOLLECTED BY WILLIAM FAULKNER

I

• • • • • *They* sat on democracy's front porch, and George put out his hand, an offered hand, in West Texas, with Barbara and the dog who was to become Mildred and the six children, warts and all, and said *I am gladdened by this day* for there was a new breeze blowing, squally and savory and resilient, and the land was covered with the pall of ashes to dust, the spent dust, powerless and which lay debilitated, and the tree blown away, and the leaves from an ancient, lifeless tree blown away, and he knew he could stoically accept or fervently vent his spleen, he dropped his reluctant fist and knew that it was not man's to do with as he pleased, and that this night was for big things, and he was talking about the truth . . . it covered all things which touch the heart—honor and pride and pity and justice and courage and love.

II

No longer the simple society of the pioneer, this split land, worked by a quiet man, a world war veteran, *I'll fight if I have to for my honor and my family*, and who said things like *don't let 'em fool ya* and *read my lips*, trying to agree, or anyway go along with, trying not to bicker, to be a kinder, gentler man, a quiet man, an idealist and a Puritan at once, he summoned the folks together, inviting and cajoling and coercing his neighbors and his friends into a house, his new house, untried unseasoned unessayed, and said *some say, you know, some say I may not be the most eloquent, I mean, but we're going to be hands-on and involved*, to build a sense of place, to work for honesty and truth and compassion against injustice and lying and greed.

III

He recited the litany of a room called Tomorrow with a window on men's souls, a part of the continuum, he wanted to add a room called Freedom (where we could summon Justice from within ourselves), where we could sleep and dream again, and watch the stars, blaze-luster beacons, a thousand and million and billion points of light, to dream an endless, enduring, yes, even a prevailing dream of the old ideas, the old truths and verities of the heart, the old ideas are new again, because they're not old, they're timeless: duty and sacrifice and commitment and love and honor and pity and pride and compassion and a patriotism that finds its expression in taking part and pitching in.

IV

George's voice roared and roared. The gavel moved again, its echo began to tap-tap steadily again, and at once the hall was quiet. Barbara glanced briefly over his shoulder, then she sat back. The American flag draped over George's fist and his eyes were bright and blue and halcyon again as sign and banner stirred smoothly once more from left to right; stage and dais, standard and flag, and placard, each in its ordered place.

—*Jane Schaffer*

BILL AND ERNIE GO FISHING

• • • • • *W*e went down from the house, over the rotting stairs, past the dying lawn, and out to the old car, itself a wood paneled anachronism that was as much a remonstrance to the town's would-be aristocracy as a re-assurance that its owner belonged among, not them, but the farmers who populated the town square each Saturday morning, selling truck crops from the backs of pickups or, mostly, playing dominoes or checkers beneath the tall statue of a Confederate officer who would forever look south when he should have been looking north.

"Drive," Ernie said.

The old Ford sighed down the hill and wheezed onto the town's main thoroughfare, past once stately antebellum homes where the black cooks and maids and gardeners still toiled as they had done for the last one hundred years for masters who for an equal amount of time had progressively squandered the money to pay them, past the rusting sign that said Abbeville was 12 miles distant, and past the old McGruder place, old man McGruder himself standing by the side of the road, the dry, billowing red clay swirling around him as we passed, a McGruder in the dust.

"Drink," Ernie grunted.

I allowed that I might break my usual code of temperance owing to the dank cold of the Yoknapatawpha river bottom where we had now arrived, the old fish camp sagging in the mud flat, and knowing that Ernie would soon empty the bottle anyway. I put on my boots, remembering the times as boy and man and libelous character I had waded these somnolent waters, whose enduring tides would always sweep these hills, endlessly, ceaselessly, to the delta below.

Suddenly, a large ten-point buck bolted from the brush. Ernie dived for the backseat of the car, erupting from the other side with a loaded shotgun we had brought for emergencies. "Yes!" he snarled. He charged into the woods. "Don't ask for whom we fell does!" Ernie shouted. "It's the bucks I want."

I followed behind, listening for the final shot and wishing I'd brought my old chum Popeye who was at least a sport if not quite as virile as Ernie. Ernie lost the deer, then found it, then lost it again, always vainly thrashing the thick black oaks and oozing yellow pines despite the clear, easy path that lay alongside. Then *crack*, and *whoomph*, and a still, sad bleat before the forest quiet descended again.

The farmer only charged us five hundred dollars for the cow Ernie shot and said he would dress it out real nice for another fifty dollars. Me, I thought about how nice it might be to take up fox hunting in Virginia.

Ernie just wanted the ears.

—*Joseph Rogers*

TROLL AT NOON

• • • • • *I*t comes again, and finally, the sound, not harsh, strident, clattering as earlier in time, that day, the morning, but blunted, heavy, ponderous, inexorable, shuddering on the boards, and presaging the catastrophe he, Troll, guessed, gleaned by now—no, knew in the somnolent blood of his thick body.

Earlier, when he lay not derelict but supine in lush red mud, the first rays of sun bronzing brown sluggish water, the first sound had roused him. That and the smell (odor), sharp, rank, penetrating even to his stomach, which, uncertain at first but then with dawning awareness in greening dawn—*not man, not mule nor horse nor wagon neither*—and soon definite, defined, and told him *goat.*

Goat? Mind wrangling, quarreling with stomach, baffled, then furious, outraged. Shaking, panting, livid, he rose, drawing with him dank fat mud, uttering sounds, words, or the equivalents—of no consequence really, inconsequential, merely adjunctive, but the grim adagio of sound requisite and incremental to the design, the pattern. His challenge, ritualistic and immemorial, and to be uttered (he did not know this then) twice more.

So the answer, confirming stomach—*goat*—but promising, enticing, leading him to postpone, delay only, not abrogate. Thus the harsh clatter recommencing over the bridge, which spanned the water, which linked the banks, and fading to unfathomable silence pure and august in the smooth transparency of time's slow shift.

Then still later, the sound, again, but stronger now, and louder his challenge (almost a wail, for he was beginning to glimpse, conjure perhaps, the design), and the answer the same so his acquiescence the more resigned, and then the silence more senescent, but the pattern the same, unchanged, thus itself the more implacable. Therefore to wait, as he had always must have known he would wait, must have known for centuries indistinct, immutable he would wait—ancient, primordial, indomitable, under bridge shading the sluggard stream. His stream, *mine and always mine and ever will be mine*, though deep and beyond that purblind, miasmal innocence he had always known it never would be such nor ever had been, the rich and fecund teeming earth denying any aspiration to ownership.

So it is now, not then, and hence, finally, the sound. *It is time*, he knows, *and not only time but Time and finally so, never to be remembered because soon I shall be Other, though I have always known I shall be other (than what I am and have been); but I always have known it and therefore* did *because knowing* is *merely remembering. For what else but this was I spawned—not mineral nor vegetable nor animal nor that cosmic mistake human—in primal ooze which has been to me not succubus but succor, rest, environ,* home. *For this only.*

So now he rises, shedding mud, warmth of sun and fresh

breath of breeze on his body, fixed, alone, serene, trium-
phant, all the past and all that ever was redundant to and
redolent of this, this *now*.

—*James L. McDonald*

THE ROUND AND THE FURRY

• • • • • *W*hen the descending sun made stripes shining through the bars, it was time to be awake and be on the wheel. When she still communicated (that was before Paula Revere), Mother had said to me, "Son, I cannot recollect whether or not you are my eldest, but I think of you as such. Always remember, Addy, that although turning the wheel should not be regarded as achieving a specific goal, the endless revolutions are in themselves a form of psychological satisfaction, dispersing a marked portion of hamster angst."

She said that, but I forgot it. I was out of the wood shavings and down the ladder from the sleep-box, and it was going round and round, my front-feet, back-feet running and running, so none of them could.

i thought Addy would be a good boy, but he bites like a cat, he once bit Bobby Trenton.

"It was because of Woody," he said.

"Nobody knew she was going to go," Ben-Frank said. He is not a golden hamster, he has a patch like his father. "You bit him before Woody went."

i often wonder whether i made her kill her babies, they say it's shock like Paula Revere. Well i was her mother, and i did not kill any of them not even J.Q. i don't remember really where they came from except it was before when Bobby put me down on the carpet and she ate me, no it wasn't me she ate it was little Teddy and Eleanor, anyway it was before that. So i stay in my wood shavings and they put the pellets very close so i dont need to get out i dont go down the ladders except to do my business in one of the corners

APPENDIX

THE HAMSTER CONDO, 1985–89.

MRS. TRENTON. An American mother. Called Mommy (and sometimes Moms), who had a son named Bobby. Who believed that pets were good for children. Who therefore urged Bobby to visit the pet store where he saw (and desired) George; who upon the realization that George was Martha purchased the Hamster Condo, a three-level residence for hamster group living; who supplied (but did not handle) the sawdust.

BOBBY TRENTON. Who with persistent maternal urging owned and attended to the residents of the Hamster Condo.

These were Hamsters:

GEORGE (MARTHA). Golden hamster of unknown provenance, who was bought as George from a pet emporium, who rapidly grew broader across her belly section, and who, upon her giving birth to Adams, J.Q., and Abigail, became Martha. Who was scared by Paula Revere and thereafter secluded and retiring.

ADAMS. Who Martha called Addy. Who was always (in hamster terms) unpredictable. Who would not let Ben-Frank go on the wheel. Who bit Bobby Trenton to his (Addy's) own satisfaction.

J.Q. Who acted fast, who loved Abigail, who died as result of consuming rhubarb leaves.

ABIGAIL. Martha's youngest offspring. Who was round and golden and smelled like greens. Who, when she first came into heat, mated with her brother J.Q. Who had seven babies; who (driven perhaps by their premature handling by Bobby Trenton) killed all seven. Who was mated by Bobby Trenton with his friend Clayton's Patch (so-called for his patch) in a stud transaction involving the negotiation of baseball cards. Who had four more babies, two of whom (Teddy and Eleanor) were eaten by Paula Revere. Who hardly seemed to notice, let alone care.

BEN-FRANK. Who had a patch like his father. Who got to the carrot peelings first. Who (unlike hamsters) thought that day was day and night was night; who, consequentially, was always on the wheel or the ladders at nap time.

WOODROW ("WOODY"). Who was loved by her uncle Addy with an admiration that was aesthetic, not sensual. Who was sent to live with Patch, in exchange for a pocket-size portrait of Reggie Jackson, and never returned to the Hamster Condo.

This was not a Hamster:
PAULA REVERE, who was a Cat.

—Clare A. Simmons

LIFE IS A LITTLE WINDY AT TIMES

• • • • • *H*e stood, inert and defunctive, just inside the front entrance to the dilapidated and rotting building *what had served quite well first as a trading post and jail and then as a cotton gin, having come down to merely being called The Gin, no doubt witnessing through time the entire story, from old Ikkemotubbe's horse swap to the final dingdong of the Snopes clan* (he thought) *back before and yes after he sold sewing machines out in Beat Four swapping lies with Quick and Armstid,* watching as the two lovebirds crossed the floor to a table, the one a man of sixty the other a girl of twenty, bringing into the room with them *perhaps it was nothing more than a recapitulation of some retroactive and defunct thread of memory from his own past* not a conviction but something close to it *that something was going to happen.* This then he told himself he had to see and crossed the same floor unnoticed, the dead and expended ambience of the place seeming to follow as he climbed the stairs to the alcove loft, a place of sanctuary for the riffraff of Yoknapatawpha County.

The bartender eyed the two suspiciously, crossing nevertheless that same floor and wiping between them, his pale reddish arm beaded with a sweat that defied credulity in the refrigerated room. He (the ex–sewing machine salesman, a

man named Radcliffe, whose forebears had called themselves Ratliff and Raycliff and Radlif and even Suratt at one
time before one of them had been forced to go to school
and find out once and for all what it really was) had known
the boy's (the bartender's) father and grandfather, better
men than he and yet themselves the watered down remnants
of a sorry clan of horse thieves and barn burners.

It (the man and the child) was, he thought, his bland
affable face still out of all sentient and biding dust relaxed,
a preposterous picture, indelible and immutable now on his
brain, that of a mindless young Helen of the cotton fields
and kudzu out to take a pathetic old man, no doubt one of
the northerners attending the Yoknapatawpha Conference.
He watched as the narrow, insubstantial butt of the bartender twitched once and froze, as he turned his insolent and
inscrutable weasel face from one of them to the other. The
two men were facing each other across the table, the one,
whose face he could see squarely, was full of outraged and
impotent insolence and the other, whose face he knew by
heart, was full of outraged insolent impotence.

This then he told himself with astonished credulity was
how it was. He descended the stairs and headed for the
front door, passing within two feet of the quarreling men,
hearing the one say to the other, "At mid-semester break
you'll have to visit us in Newark. Temple June has talked
about nobody and no thing but you for a year." And the
other, with a happy twitch of his behind, saying, "Y'all kin
bet Ah will do thet."

—*Wesley E. Hall*

A Wal-Mart For Jefferson

• • • • • *F*irst was the nameless plot of land: doomed to be encompassed in the apotheosis of the white man's trade; transmogrified by the hands of man from its moiling earthface, gully-drawn plow-turned ammoniac mule-ambulated; its immortal destiny to be parking-lotted and Wal-Marted; where the once indomitable trees fell to the ax and the horny-handed (and nameless now too) sons of the earth: they myriad and mired and miscegenated and more—mixed up—who thought that by having they could own when owning wasnt possessing, omitting the apostrophe of doom from their possessive pronouns and even contractions, but rather fraught imperiled charged laden and plumb stuck with—blest and damned too—damned too the sons of the sons of the horny-handed now murmuring in the now air-conditioned Courthouse in Jefferson: "Let him take it. I cant farm it. Maybe that Walton can grow one of his big stores there." This last said with a derisive laugh. So thus came Walton or rather an attorney of Walton's, *quorum pars magna fui* ("With a lot more 'phooey' than 'magna,' a Ratliff quipped), Memphis-slick in a suit looking machine-stamped from tin, or tinned from a stamp-machine, or something like that; at least that was the talk as the myriad town voices witnessed the deal closed; and the Jefferson women choruslike and absolved from abhorrence in their modern assent: they too doomed but not damned—undamned yet not undone, the granddaughters of they who once would rage unsilently at the sight of Grant on a fifty-dollar bill, refusing to accept one from a bank in that spinal severity that not '63 nor '64 nor '65 could snap; overnight and timeless the big store rose; they all shopped there; some of their sons and daughters even worked there (though one said, this a Ratliff again, he "could never actively flush one when he was hunting for one") myriad in the aisles, each item in its ordered place, where now nothing smelled where long ago once the aspirant shopper inhaled the earthy kerosene and cheese smells and man-odors of the general store. Now no more; gone, doomed, damned—Wal-Mart.

—*Michael A. Crivello*

THE PAIR

• • • • • *S*he realized that it had begun a long time before. It had already begun on the day that she first wrote her weight in three digits and her mother—eyes rolling and luminous and no sound only that effluvium of something more than bitch, marked her with the epitome and apotheosis of an ancient dread abhorrence—the worst name of all—of the woman juxtaposed and crudely reliefed against the definitive designation of divinity—*The Porker.* She had already encompassed the long legend of pantries rifled, of scones and carrot cake and even corn dogs carried stealthily into her room and devoured and brassieres and bloomers outgrown and matriarchal warnings and even insults delivered in weighty and deliberate exactitude—a chronicle of an anachronism of woman-child fatuous enough to believe that plenteous pulchritude could prevail in a doomed wilderness of women constantly gnawed at by men with tape measures and scales.

Her day came at last. They met not in pursuit of lust but in relinquishment. He—son of a Swampscott socialite and the great-great-grandson of an Aztec anchorite, who abhorred the chattel and relentless thrall of a land in which all the ancient rules of flesh and fecundity had been abrogated, entered with her into a fluid yet intact circumambience. They dreamed of a new land, palpable, inviolable, a substantial bequeathment to their descendants who would not inherit repudiation and impotence but rather humility and pride.

So it began: he felt the whole enveloping weight of her—then the whisper, the promise of love, and incredible amplitude, an enveloping composite of all woman-flesh. Like avatars of a cosmic primordial galactic marsh, they rode the isolate sea of their warmed, fecund water bed, until washed up on the insatiate immemorial beach—mammalian, leviathan, mythic mergings of the pariah-hood of obesity and the cajolery of indomitability.

That was all. They would never need listen to lies again: the implacable succession of voices in a voluble inflexible catechism, repudiating the boundless glory of flesh, exuding a wondrous rapacity. Their deliverance, like a portent, echoed the sonorous message—"forever panting, forever young"—the breathless murmurings of the "solid flesh" of immortality. They would learn of Titian and Rubens and trust the evocation of that comprehensive girth in their repudiation of slim and trim. For they knew now that what pumped the heart, spewing the dregs of plaque before a passionate wash of adrenalized force would not only prevail but endure. They were vindicated.

—Joan Fedor

LIGHT IN THE MALL

• • • • • *I*f I could only see," he thought, thought turning in on itself amorphous, brooding, opaque, thought-not-thought anymore, ceasing to be thought, ceasing to be the be-ness of being itself, no longer identifiable, but vague—vague and shadowless, like shadows which themselves have fled the shadows of their very being, shamed among the shamed, pitiful among the pitiful, hopeless to the very apogee of hopelessness, the very dingdong of doom in a vast gloom-filled swamp that is swamp-mud-vague-squishing-cold-against-the-feet of his subconscious mind, squishing cold cold wet, timeless, the hidden horror of generations of doomed mud moving, inexorably, toward their final, inevitable twilight.

"If I could only see the sky," he thought, his impotent rage somehow not rage anymore but rather surrender; cold, resonant, complete, but still somehow not not-rage.

But he couldn't see the sky.

He worked at the stationery store in the mall (enclosed as they all were, even the ones in the north he had heard, with its lighted ceiling, lighted even though the low sun of a slate sky, gaugeless, eternal, unforgiving, merciless, and doomed, burned coldly with a hard orange indifference outside where the air was not yet cleansed of the glory and shame and immensity of a past so distant, yet so unrelenting, so merciless, eternal).

Grind, grind, grind.

To his left, the other salesclerk, Cash, was cutting a duplicate house key for Addie Christmas, because her son Joe had fed the original key to their cow who thought its mother was a fish.

"My mother's a cow-fish," it thought.

"All in the world I want is to be left alone," he thought, rage-not-rage-now, sweat breaking out on his brow, sweat not from the unknowable nothingness of the darkest deep but rather the sweat of dread anticipation, the dread of knowing, not knowing, then knowing again, that the man in the shapeless blue-gray coverallslike suit was going to walk to his register to pay for the black felt pen the man held in his upraised left hand as he strode deliberately, unconsciously (for how could it be otherwise?) toward the clerk like a ghost, long-dead, not waiting to hear the bugle call of a failed cavalry advance where the sweat and the blood and the smoke of battle were timeless, frozen, and inescapable even in this neon-lighted hell of a franchised stationery store in this generic suburban shopping mall, in an equally generic suburban neighborhood that once was cotton fields and hay fields and tobacco fields of an ethereal and eternal South: Proud, damned, haunted, paved-over.

The man, faceless although he had a face; only faceless because the clerk dare not look at it for reasons equally compelling and unfathomable, placed the black marker pen on the faded green counter.

"All in the world I want is to be left alone," the clerk thought.

"That's all I want. I get off in an hour, I make minimum wage, I have no benefits, and what in the world do I care, although I know I probably should, whether or not this man buys this felt-tip pen? Why can't he buy it from Cash?"

Grind, grind, grind.

"All in the world I want is to be left alone," he thought.

"Will that be all?" he asked absently, dead somehow already.

"Yes."

"Cash or charge?"

"Cash."

—Don Mangan

GO DOWN, BOLPHRAM

*I*n that four o'clock is earlier than six, which the young man considered undeniably early, Bolphram fell conscious again very early that chill morning. His grandma had risen from the bed in the other room with the aid of the metal cane that sprouted legs on the bottom and crossed to the rocking chair in the adjoining kitchen and, sitting there at length, started her morning prayers in a furious whisper that had, word by word, returned him to awareness of the tissue, if that, staving off the cold from his calves.

And by now he had seen her negotiate the cot again and then the rocking chair, pass the kitchen table juxtaposed against the crystal cabinet and, aided still by the length of metal with sprouting legs, enter the bathroom turning the switch on sending forth a stabbing point of white brilliance into Bolphram's now open eyes revealing simultaneously the floor-length light blue translucent nightgown draped upon her enormous elastic breasts beneath the curly white-yellow of her hair and the glasses. As he watched further, squinting, she closed the door; he could hear the sound of impact as the door rebounded against a box on the floor, wedging it there negligently, and the wash of brilliance ebbed away.

And for an expanse of minutes now, he heard nothing more from the bathroom. He suspected that she might be reading. He doubted himself, however, in the way that he had grown accustomed to doubting himself. For a time, this was all right, because his doubting was as much a manifestation of habit as of anything else, but the sound of his own breathing was beginning to consume the contents of his awareness. Huff huff huff huff. Dont it grow old to be there, still, on the can? The thought of *old* formed phantoms of decrepitude in his mind which danced and flew between the spaces of brilliance, asking him, or even begging him, to come, see, discover what had been severed from the scope of his vision. No, she was all right, he told himself several times.

Finally, Bolphram can take no more. Launching himself, he reduces the threshold and kitchen and all the vastness of a few steps into one more decisive inhalation of air. And Bolphram steps backward—one leg back and one bent forward—and then propels himself with all his might against the wooden frame and all that bars his passage, and then there is a sudden evacuation of pressure before him and then splinters and dust that clogs his nasal cavities such that for one distended moment he is gagging before the open space returns and then more and more open space until finally he is falling or tumbling in space as an acrobat might, and suddenly the sound and the furious choreography end with one wrenching lurch that all but dislocates femur from pelvis.

There on the throne, she is petrified.

"I need to go to the bathroom," he says.

—Mark Moran

INCLUSION IN THE RUST

•　•　•　•　•　*M*argolis lay on his back in the stinking mud of Westchester County contemplating the underside of the black BMW that had favored him with so many moments of pleasure and satisfaction. He could neither comprehend (the mystery of) its complete and sudden failure as the ineluctable outcome of myriad less urgent (ignored) warnings nor associate the failure of the vehicle with the imminent catastrophe awaiting its owner. Gazing up out of the detritus of a half century of affluent nomads on this the southbound Merritt Parkway, noting the tired latex jetsam of long-ago couplings in this abandoned service area and perhaps even himself noticed by the grown-up products of these couplings passing him now at high speed, he could not have appreciated, could not even have imagined that the tiny flawed kernel embedded in a casting years ago at the Krupp factory an ocean away had found its way, through failures, meltings, recastings, and more meltings, into the crankshaft of his vehicle. The failure, slow in coming, was complete as he would discover somewhat later at the dealership in Scarsdale, but somewhat before the discovery that as he had driven past Norwalk and North Stamford and

Greenwich and White Plains his wife of twenty years was packing for her final departure. Later he was to remember that morning that final immutable morning as one on which the *Wall Street Journal* had failed to come and on which, as he and his wife had passed in the narrow darkness of the hall by the bedroom, each had moved away, saying, "Excuse me."

Now he got up and brushed at his coat absently and looked south toward New York. "Damn," he said.

—E. M. McMahon, Jr.

As I Sat Typing

• • • • • *O*n the table the lean jaw of the typewriter sat in gaping unamaze like a memento mori, a death's head that stared at the writer sitting in undaunted authorial pride, his fingers poised above the keys so that he (the writer) looked not monklike or afraid but like a concert pianist awaiting silence, ignoring completely the omen on the table. A bottle of corn whiskey stood at his feet corked like a genie or a djinni though he would rather have had a whiskey than a djinni and had no use at all for a genie, conjuring out of his own tarnished and magical chamber figures fantastic and chimerical that appeared on the page in mythical procession.

The writer regarded the as yet un-noveled page with keen eyes, patient and determined but weary too, the mouth drawn under the gray mustache that had belonged to his grandfather, Colonel Beowolf Falkner, who had ridden savage and furious and completely hairless out of the indomitable hills of Virginia and into an old Chikasaw barbershop where he had pulled it off the face of another man with main force and ridden out again without even paying, and though his beard and sideburns, which he had also stolen, had been shot off at Bull Run, had preserved and passed down the old growth of facial hair as a token and a promise, though of what no one was sure.

The hands hanging poised and tireless over the old Royal fell now incorporate on the lettered keys, moving with purposeful digitation, the carriage seeming to move and return in self-willed repetition like the roll of a player piano though the only music was the tick tick tick of the typewriter like time itself tapping out against the white field of death the letters and words that alone could stain the shroudlike imbecile blankness of the page.

But then the writer stopped. He pulled the white page from the clenched teeth of the machine and the machine fell silent as if he had ripped its tongue out too along with the paper and the only sound was the crumpling of paper until that too fell silent and his hand held the light ball like a tiny skull, gripping it the way the first man gripped the first primitive tool, holding prehensile in dim Cro Magnitude the harsh stone, the petrified invention, or mere accident only that might kill or perhaps dig a hole or whittle a stick or carve the first picture on the first cave black and recessed, the australopithecine rendering of a mastodon or a mule. He (the writer) brandished the paper and threw it like Adam tossing away the apple, half eaten, throwing it not with anger or disgust but with furious resignation until it flew through the writer's room and seemed to hang, tideless and eternal, before landing in the corner with the rest of the white trash. But he did not see it land for he had already turned his back and sat typing once more.

—Jonathan Rosen

YOKNAPATAWPHA DREAMING

• • • • • *S*o, less for love of judicature than the need for sustenance, he lawyered weekdays upstairs on the square over the (long-vacant) chiropractor's office and circumperspicated, between deeds, from his window over the hundred and fifty years of college students who came to study lust and idleness and learned—though grudgingly and with some remorse—much else; then Saturdays, alone in his ten acres of woods, relict of his grandfather's and his father's half section, thirty-odd years asylum to such worthless and unrepentant species as might voluntarily grow there (a Snopes would call this tree farming, otherwise not) among the old rows and terraces and the futile and rusty barbwire, its fungus-crumbled unperpendicularity slackly setting off once-field from once-pasture—though by now it was all the same. And he had axed out trails by hand among the privet and devil's club, impermeably laced and Gordian-bound with thickets of honeysuckle and muscadine then at first God-scattering random wildflowers and fern spores only to find that none grew, and starting over again and again, wrenching them, the ferns, up from the loathsome snout-defiled soil by plain bovine will as his grandfather had tried to wrench nickel cotton or Sutpen his mansion (though none remembered the mansion or Sutpen and few his grandfather) and often they fed the bugs and cutworms or got dug up by armadillos and (himself gnawed upon by every genus and family of arthropod able to consume flesh or drink blood that could endure the taste of him, Sundays dogged by pain and fatigue, Mondays overcome by an abiding darkness) he would, come another weekend, be back in the woods, summer or winter, the seasons precessing seamlessly, a melancholy pageant of golds and greens and browns; until time justified his grim confidence that he could grow them all: where first Varner mules, then his grandfather's, had plodded and strained (bastard ears flicking for news of the evening mill whistle down at Frenchman's Bend) woodfern and chainfern, Woodsias and Alabama lipfern adapted and flourished, then sensitive ferns, bracken, serendipitous Scott's spleenworts, autumn cardinal flowers scattering of bloodroot and catchfly—and with every new introduction, his orphan law practice dwindled.

It was all vanity, a monument to impermanence and transience. Even though he might forestall the chain saws and the bulldozers —might, by artifice, hold back the (omnivorous) amoeboid and mindless metastasis of parking lots and video arcades, the primeval, obliterating all-consuming lifeless shade must then hold sway; it was all vanity, all transience, but he could ask no more than odds (cosmic at that) for there to remain in that distant postmillennium, when the red oaks, sweet gums, and tulip poplars fell and rotted, the site scoured by flame and winter rain, that single unconquerable spore, unwinding prothallial threads down into the ash-littered, newly fertile soil, reborn to light, to replenish and colonize, find a niche and endure, leaving him, like Abraham, father to pteridophytic multitudes down the brooding and unfathomable ages.

—Samuel Tumey

ABBOTT, ABBOTT!

• • • • • *A*nd by the time he (the old man) surrendered himself to what for him (the judge) appeared as nothing but a manifestation of the necessity imparted on them by a century's design beyond anything conceivable as will or choice or even the momentary caprice of some long-forgotten but still present architect, there was no turning back, no rediscovering within themselves the vital source of this grim vicissitude which took the form of the old man's scrawled arrangement of names possessed by him (the millionaire) yet not now nor ever the property of any man but rather free agents in an inescapable dialogue between nondescript men (the lawyers) for whom nothing mattered but the eventual recompense taken as their due: the commission, contested in close rooms filled with the guilty refuse of tobacco (this was before the surgeon general) and in anticipation of an early evening's mastication *because we have credit cards* and you wanted to strike them but could not for fear of retribution, though even lacking this fear—this genuflection before the unstated superiority of their (the lawyers') ratiocination—you would be striking not a real man but the ghost of the long-dead Abner, absent yet present in the very design whose joy had turned to resignation in the hands of gamblers and gluttons and thieves." He paused.

"For God's sake!" the other implored. "Go on!"

"The judge, armored in the vestments of his trade, the thick black cushion upon his chest, the matrix of wire and rubber covering like a mask what was for him itself a mask, and lower the concave plastic cup preserving the possibility of his lineage beyond this temporary suspension in an unreal landscape whose origin was no more nor less than that of the ubiquitous Abner (Abner), the judge facing fresh judgments gaining on him with the inevitable speed of maturity, remembering Grandfather, removed from this world like a string on a banjo past tuning, giving him the lie in the form of a deliberately bad call on that afternoon he had forever lost his innocence and understood gracelessly that the rules of the game were not there as eternal verities but merely conveniently shared falsehoods to be taken up and abandoned as dark necessity required. And he took the card from the other's hand." The remote look again emerged in the speaker's eye, registering past and present and future collapsed into one crumpled index card whose dim nervous scribbles held not redemption but that unspoken tragedy rooted in what had seemed an interminable misunderstanding between the two absent yet present men now perceived only in memory. The other, barely able to contain the madness provoked by this ineffable parallel of present and past, snatched the card away, adjusting his eyes to the low light of the room no longer filled by the dust motes dancing in noon's inexpressible shafts, and read from the uppermost line: "Who," he whispered. "Who was on first."

—*Jimm Erickson*

The Swing and the Caddie

*I*t was the South in all its inestimable shattered fury, raging on in the light of August, the green-ribboned paths between the flags raking the dust of his imagination and causing him to see them filled with gray marching men.

"Hit's yore shot, Lute," said Cash, "But you cain't shoot from there. Hit wouldn't be right."

"That sand trap's nigh enough the cup t'be chewin on it," said Lute. "But it don't confront me. Let ere a man say I don't begrudge it. The Lord giveth. It'd be her wish."

He moved back to the men's tee with a dull incomprehending obedience, at once alert and implacable in his slow but irreversible forward motion.

Rulon spat in the dust by the ball washer.

"Damn," he said. "Damn."

Lute gazed out onto the fairway and saw Lafe bellowing by the willow tree, untended and glorious in his ablution of himself, raging as the corn-colored sun set over the fields, and bales of dolorous cotton stood precariously by, as if in faltering defiance of the surrender of Lee at Appomattox Courthouse, emblems of a South that still breathed, because the fact that *it shouldn't have happened* had changed with age to the fact that *it didn't happen.*

The air smelled of wisteria as if from a scent immersed in a time before this, when a sense of righteousness existed and obviated a need to rely on the spurious conflagrations of a world that had already proved itself insane and had seen its best and noblest buried by a barren, fieldless road near Gettysburg or Chickamauga. That had brought about the whole process of Colonel Lavoris's death, who had survived the war to return to an irrevocably gaunt existence in a changed world and decided from that moment, perhaps even from the iron gray moment he heard of Lee's surrender, that he would never play golf again.

And she, living with him for more than thirty years without knowing why they had never golfed, to find out in the impenetrable, breathless shimmering of an already sweltering early morning at the course by the hamlet where they had seen the spotted horses, unvanquished in their tenuous captivity. She knew from the very moment that she decided to go into the town (the moments between it and the point in the afternoon when she was arrested for shooting a man on the street assuming a palsied slowness, as if somehow weighted physically by the air heavy with loss, as the shadow cast longingly by the statue of the Confederate soldier moved with the descent of the sun, abrogating the golden silence of the square) that she would kill him.

So the son grew up with greens privileges that had been delivered from the womb of a past written in fury and paid for in blood, that ineffable moment etched in his mind when his grandson found the pistol, now rusted and seeming, as he hefted it, to have gained weight with its unrelenting presence in a world where it made no sense.

He moved his feet back and forth in the black shoes that seemed to have been cut from solid tar and prepared to drive the absurd white sphere into a past he hated.

"Fore, I reckon!" he said, shouting it because he knew he had to, but at the same time silent in his unrelenting abasement of a game he considered foolish.

—John C. Richards

Sampson Agonistes*

．．．．． *S*o the embattlement came in the fifth game when Sampson (the name given, not chosen) flung an annihilating fist at Jerry Sichting (intended, not achieved) and so was ejected and banished from the game (saying, "a bullshit call, a bullshit call"); Sampson whose corporeal verticality peaked not at five and a half, not at six and a half, but at seven and a half feet, the frame towering, immense, monumental, yet neither hefty nor profuse in the sinew and tissue and primordial beef that had made Moses Malone such an indomitable leader in Houston four years before; he (Sampson) whose inexorable progress up court was impeded not forthrightly with a stationary screen but demonically with hostile movement from below, who felt his body (light and august) badgered not for the first time and not by accident, who was badgered even at U.V.A. where seven feet four inches and gifted should win not some, not most, but all games, swinging not at Jerry Sichting

---

* Faulkner's account of the brief fight between Ralph Sampson and Jerry Sichting during the fifth game of the 1986 N.B.A. championship series between the Houston Rockets and the Boston Celtics.

(at six feet one inch was no taller than many of the sporting scribes who tormented him in Virginia and who tormented him now) but at all life's insidious entanglements and diminutive fatalities; and then he lay sighing in the forced sanctuary of the locker room, watching the TV image outraged (Sampson not on the court, Sampson not playing), thinking "It was done for no reason, done to spite and flout me, as if I were not Sampson (light and august) but some nameless reserve putting in two minutes, then yanked"; yet I hold no brief for Sampson, responding afterward (the game over and won) with upraised fist (triumph as well as anger now) to the sound and the fury of the impassioned home crowd, knowing even then that he must return to Boston where the twin pillars (Olajuwon the other) would surely collapse, vanquished at last.

—Jeffrey E. Simpson

THE ITTY-BITTY PLACE

BOOK ONE: SLIM

• • • • • *A*s he watched Jumpy Varnish haul his oblivious sister on horseback to and from school every day, he had only one thought but would have expressed it to no man even would they have asked it of him, which in their backwoods clannish Baptist Democrat pride they would not, nor even if he could have spit it out, which in the unintelligible obtuseness of his hill-bred nonverbosity he could not. Instead, he chewed.

BOOK TWO: HULA

Jiggling attractively to school every morning would have been her idea of hell if she had bothered to have ideas, to let the long recording of mankind's temporal and fleeting struggles with his doom enter her head at all, or even had she bothered to wake up, to open wide those eyes like mammalian monstrosities stained beneath the satyr's trampled hothouse grapes long enough to notice either the jiggling or the attractiveness or even the horse. Instead, she snored.

BOOK THREE: THE OTHERS

Will Varnish was an irascibly jolly old man of thirty or eighty with between two and sixteen children, depending on what year the author counted them up in. He held simultaneously every elected and appointed post, Baptist and Democrat, in this part of the county short of pooper-scooper, which with exemplary paternal concern and pure unadulterated foresight he had delegated to his son Jumpy, and ran the only combination general store and sawmill in American literature, whose sign read Have Lumber Will Varnizh, belying not so much his interest in the business he would one day bequeath his numberless progeny and not even really so much his illimitable and maybe even boundless self-esteem but rather the absolute stranglehold he had on the pursuits, economic spiritual sexual and trivial, of the itty-bitty place.

BOOK FOUR: THE LIFELONG BUMMER

When Will Varnish needed a husband for the hugely outrageously and somnolently pregnant Hula, Slim Sniflet was chewing, implacable.

"What more do you want?" Varnish said, cried, and otherwise demanded. "She'll never wake up long enough to get in your way, and I've already said I'll pay for a maid and a cook and a French architect to build you that house in town with the columns outside and the special shelf on the mantel for you to rest your boots on the inside. What else on God's earth could you possibly want?"

With each inexorably passing cumulatively irrevocable second of Slim's inviolable unreply, Varnish began surely and with certainty to get ready to regret forever the anguish he was doomed to suffer because never as long as he lived would he ever have the chance opportunity to fling or even throw hard the carefully selected and now tragically un-hurled poetical epithets (*usurper*, *Brutus*, *Mephistopheles*, *jerk*) in the face of his nemesis; never thus to alter however slightly the encroaching course of Sniflet and his concomi-tant *-ism* in Unpronounceable County; never to embody unflagging mortal man's sententious dubiousness: never. Instead, he repeated the question.

Slim spat. "That sure is a jewel of a horse," he said.

—Teresa Towner

BRAN BURNING

• • • • • *T*he kitchen in which Phlegm Snopes held family court smelled of rye husks baking on a tray in the oven. The boy raised his skinny rump from the chair to smell the hulls baking at 325 degrees. He could see through the square of glass into the oven, and though he could not read the recipe on the counter—the black lettering meant nothing to him, like history—he knew he smelled in the steady wash of warm air and unwashed family another smell, a scent of fear and decay and grief—for he was a full-blooded Snopes, blind to the truth and chained to the past whether he knew it or not—and the rush of blood to his head made him woozy like his brothers Heck and I.O.U., who were anxious to confess their guilt and leave the kitchen (where no good ever originated, not the way their mother cooked) and run to town for Coca-Colas and Ding Dongs and some conversation at Homer Barren's 7–11 (which was only open 9:00 A.M. till 7:00 P.M., when Homer went home for supper), but their father would not let up, not for one minute, for he fancied himself wise as Solomon who never put to death an honest man, for who among us is honest or ever was, 'cept Him Who died on the cross?

Heck and I.O.U. wanted to confess but their father would not quit talking, harping like King David of Israel, and the smell of the burning husks hit the boy like an errant Roman candle set off by mistake and headed straight for the outhouse and what could he do outside his head when within he thought *Ourn rye husks is overcooked!* but bite his lip and think *I will have to do hit!*

"I don't figure to preach all day and all night 'bout this theft," the boy's father was saying, his voice cold as December and harsh and flat, "but if the heirloom ain't returned to me before the cock crows, you boys be two pounds lighter from the loss of blood and other bodily fluids." There, he had had his say; like the Lord on the seventh day, he rested.

"I confess," Heck said, not raising his eyes. He was honest enough when you threatened him with pain or prison.

"Me too," said I.O.U. in a whisper. "We took the damn thing and traded it to Miss Lula's boy Turl for a lottery ticket—"

"Turned out to be used," Heck felt compelled to add.

"You stole my favored can opener!" their father screamed. "My own boys, thieves!"

"Jew think somebody broke int' the house to steal your can opener, Pap?" Heck asked.

Smoke from the oven escaped; no one noticed but the boy. He had to do something, now. The husks would burn black, ruined and useless.

"Bran!" the boy cried. "Bran!"

His mother and father, his two older brothers, the birds and dogs and the wind in the trees—they all stopped. The world stopped spinning for a full second, until their mother spoke up.

"He talked! The boy can talk!"

"Bah!" the boys' father said, disgusted. "Now we got to name him."

The boys' mother stood to turn off the oven but paused, swollen with maternal triumph, and smiling with all the enduring liquid bovine tenderness of her sex, she told her youngest son: "I always knew maybe you'd talk."

They say Bran Snopes never spoke another word until his dying day, when he asked the preacher, "Is that bran I smell burnin'?" But the preacher, a man who never knew when to say quit and do it, told Bran that he reckoned it was all the souls of all the Snopeses burning in hell that Bran smelled, and wasn't that a shame when it's such a simple thing to confess your sins and be saved from eternal death and damnation, but it was too late: Bran had died about two lines back. It was the syntax that sent Bran Snopes to everlasting perdition, not the sin itself.

—John Ruemmler

As We Go Walking

. . . . . *A*gain that morning he commenced the trek, the peregrination, without illusion but also without hope of personal gain or coffee—though earlier, before the commencing even, he had doubtless rankled at, cursed perhaps, the dread intractable ritual of his dawn.

"Let's go," he said. "It's freezing."

From the stoop the poodle gazed at him in wordless canine paradox, as if in peevish acknowledgment of its own capitulation and servitude, its runny nostrils violating the air with fierce, antic jets of condensation. Suddenly, abruptly, without warning, the dog descended gingerly to the icy sidewalk.

Because this morning would be different, though they did not know that yet, had not the slightest idea even. And not just because of the cold, the weather, the elemental meteorological fact of an arctic front which without point or apparent purpose or stint had swept into their lives unheralded like some inscrutable elastic odor and which at some future time would just as unceremoniously blow off. No: because if anything, it—the inexplicable defiance which lay mere moments ahead, lurked rather, loomed too—

would reveal that quality of random inevitability which has little or nothing at all to do with the weather.

So that was when the poodle walked right around it, the plug, the hydrant rising peremptory, mute, and inviolate from the mottled curb; but not even around it, simply past it, without sniffing even: its, the pet's, tail bolt upright, its shorn head erect and poised like an extravagant appendage or aberrant vegetable upon the furious spindle of its neck, its trunk and belly bound by the pink knit sweater and motionless save for the giddy churning of its repudiant paws.

"What is it, Quentin?" he said. "Quentin? Not this, the walking, but the other, the hydrant's implacable dispossession? No. All right," he said. "Yes. Because you can't." *Won't*, he thought, *out of some stubborn fealty of species, or outraged begrudgement of blood or temperament or quirk.* "Would too, wouldn't you," he said, "today of all days?"

Quentin, still moving, cocked his ears in rakish and quizzical riposte. His eyes were the color of wet galoshes. And suddenly he was there, already standing by it, the gnarled leggy wisteria clambering leafless above the browned-out lawn in defunctive apotheosis (a vine which had prevailed not only as a symbol of the block, the street, the neighborhood association to which just this year he, the owner of a solitary pet, had been elected secretary-treasurer, but as an emblem too, a testament, to the endless tedium and exacerbation of yard work).

The act, the deed itself—the ancient immemorial effluvium—lasted only for an instant. *Because time was*, he thought, *is*, watching Quentin hover in graceful and immortal equipoise, *the static immolation of all custom, confounding even itself in the plangent echo of its clang.*

"Good boy," he said. Because the two of them, owner and pet alike, could hurry home now out of the inexorable tyranny of cold—and once again, he realized, doubtless endure.

—*David Impastato*

THE SOUND AND THE FURY
APPENDIX II

• • • • • *W*ILLIAM FAULKNER. Great-grand-son of a Southern writer. Inherited a surname which he enlarged and tempered when on his return from service with a foreign air force (he had piloted warplanes over France, he told some, and afterward army surgeons had fitted a silver plate into his skull) he took to writing. Whose prentice works were hand-lettered efforts in drama and poesy and bad short stories in Sunday newspapers published downriver in New Orleans where he had gone with his typewriter and his aspiration and with very little else. Dismissed from his position as Ol' Miss postmaster (he had "mistreated mail of all classes," wrote the postal inspector, not knowing then about the art) and found other work as sometime power-plant night-shift roustabout and university golfcoursegroundskeeper, but not before he had conceived and begun to translate, tame, and order (engrave and print and to distribute, if you will) what he would call his own small postage stamp of native soil meaning thereby the fictional acreage which he would christen and hallow as Yoknapatawpha County. Sojourned in Hollywood and pedlarwise sold detective stories to the *Saturday Evening Post* and sojourned yet again in Hollywood, glittering brightest among that constellation of impecunious novelists who were Howard Hawks's screenwriters, and yet in all this never compromised that studied aloof detached air which found its apogee in true (some) and apocryphal (others) tales of eccentric and sometimes even taciturn seclusion. Who (as he in re-creating his own name had lengthened simple vowel into diphthong) hammered out a syntax and diction and general novelistic style which outstripped capacity of thesaurus or simple dictionary and often even the skill of a well-paid copy editor and which were (the syntax, style, and diction) the outward and visible signs of a fiction which refashioned a history and present until in their apotheosis they were the fictional landmarks which had become the referents and the real-life towns and homes and rivers which were now the items to be studied and interpreted so that professionals and plainspoken afficionados alike would ride about his county in rented cars and air-conditioned buses. But who long before then, in that year which marked the midpoint and balancing fulcrum of his century, had achieved his own apotheosis (a medal; a speech: accolades of a Nordic capital) and long since had abandoned his tales of aerial combat and silver plate and in their stead declared that he was just a farmer who wrote. "I'm just a farmer who writes," he said. That sentence was his simplest fiction.

—*Allen D. Boyer*

The Smokehouse

●●●●●

SELECT FAULKNER PARODIES
FROM THE PAST

REQUIEM FOR A NOUN,
OR INTRUDER IN THE DUSK

• • • • • *T*he cold brussels sprout rolled off the
page of the book I was reading and lay inert and defunctive
in my lap. Turning my head with a leisure at least three-
fourths impotent rage, I saw him standing there holding
the toy with which he had catapulted the vegetable, or rather
the reverse, the toy first then the fat insolent fist clutching
it and then above that the bland defiant face beneath the
shock of black hair like tangible gas. It, the toy, was one
of those cardboard funnels with a trigger near the point for
firing a small celluloid ball. Letting the cold brussels sprout
lie there in my lap for him to absorb or anyhow apprehend
rebuke from, I took a pull at a Scotch highball I had had
in my hand and then set it down on the end table beside
me.

"So instead of losing the shooter which would have been
a mercy you had to lose the ball," I said, fixing with a stern
eye what I had fathered out of all sentient and biding dust;
remembering with that retroactive memory by which we
count chimes seconds and even minutes after they have
struck (recapitulate, even, the very grinding of the bowels
of the clock before and during and after) the cunning furtive

click, clicks rather, which perception should have told me then already were not the trigger plied but the icebox opened. "Even a boy of five going on six should have more respect for his father if not for food," I said, now picking the cold brussels sprout out of my lap and setting it—not dropping it, setting it—in an ashtray; thinking how across the wax bland treachery of the kitchen linoleum were now in all likelihood distributed the remnants of string beans and cold potatoes and maybe even tapioca. "You're no son of mine."

I took up the thread of the book again or tried to: the weft of legitimate kinship that was intricate enough without the obbligato of that dark other: the sixteenths and thirty-seconds and even sixty-fourths of dishonoring cousinships brewed out of the violable blood by the ineffaceable errant lusts. Then I heard another click; a faint metallic rejoinder that this time was neither the trigger nor the icebox but the front door opened and then shut. Through the window I saw him picking his way over the season's soiled and sun-frayed vestiges of snow like shreds of rotted lace, the cheap upended toy cone in one hand and a child's cardboard suit-case in the other, toward the road.

I dropped the book and went out after him who had forgotten not only that I was in shirtsleeves but that my braces hung down over my flanks in twin festoons. "Where are you going?" I called, my voice expostulant and forlorn on the warm numb air. Then I caught it: caught it in the succinct outrage of the suitcase and the prim churning rear and marching heels as well: I had said he was no son of mine, and so he was leaving a house not only where he was not wanted but where he did not even belong.

"I see," I said in that shocked clarity with which we perceive the truth instantaneous and entire out of the very astonishment that refuses to acknowledge it. "Just as you now cannot be sure of any roof you belong more than half under, you figure there is no housetop from which you might not as well begin to shout it. Is that it?"

Something was trying to tell me something. Watching him turn off on the road—and that not only with the ostensible declaration of vagabondage but already its very assumption, attaining as though with a single footfall the very apotheosis of wandering just as with a single shutting of a door he had that of renunciation and farewell—watching him turn off on it, the road, in the direction of the Permisangs', our nearest neighbors, I thought *Wait; no; what I said was not enough for him to leave the house on; it must have been the blurted inscrutable chance confirmation of something he already knew, and was half able to assess, either out of the blown facts of boyhood or pure male divination or both.*

"What is it you know?" I said springing forward over the delicate squalor of the snow and falling in beside the boy. "Does any man come to the house to see your mother when I'm away, that you know of?" Thinking *We are mocked, first by the old mammalian snare, then, snared, by the final uni-laterality of all flesh to which birth is given; not only not knowing when we may be cuckolded, but not even sure that in the veins of the very bantling we dandle does not flow the miscreant sniggering wayward blood.*

"I get it now," I said, catching in the undeviating face just as I had in the prim back and marching heels the steady articulation of disdain. "Cuckoldry is something of which the victim may be as guilty as the wrong-doers. That's what you're thinking? That by letting in this taint upon our heritage I am as accountable as she or they who have been its actual avatars. More. Though the foe may survive, the sleeping sentinel must be shot. Is that it?"

"You talk funny."

Mother-and-daughter blood conspires in the old mammalian office. Father-and-son blood vies in the ancient phallic enmity. I caught him by the arm and we scuffled in the snow. "I will be heard," I said, holding him now as though we might be dancing, my voice intimate and furious against the furious sibilance of our feet in the snow. Thinking how revelation had had to be inherent in the very vegetable scraps to which venery was probably that instant contriving to abandon me, the cold boiled despair of whatever already featureless suburban Wednesday Thursday or Saturday supper the shot green was the remainder. "I see another thing," I panted, cursing my helplessness to curse whoever it was had given him blood and wind. Thinking *He's glad; glad to credit what is always secretly fostered and fermented out of the vats of chidhood fantasy anyway (for all childhood must conceive a substitute for the father that has conceived it (finding that other inconceivable?); thinking He is walking in a nursery fairy tale to find the king his sire.* "Just as I said to you 'You're no son of mine' so now you answer back 'Neither are you any father to me.' "

The scherzo of violence ended as abruptly as it had begun. He broke away and walked on, after retrieving the toy he had dropped and adjusting his grip on the suitcase which he had not, this time faster and more urgently.

———

The last light was seeping out of the shabby sky, after the hemorrhage of sunset. High in the west where the fierce constellations soon would wheel, the evening star in single bombast burned and burned. The boy passed the Permisangs' without going in, then passed the Kellers'. Maybe he's heading for the McCullums', I thought, but he passed their house too. Then he, we, neared the Jelliffs'. He's got to be going there, his search will end there, I thought. Because that was the last house this side of the tracks. And because *something was trying to tell me something.*

"Were you maybe thinking of what you heard said about Mrs. Jelliff and me having relations in Spuyten Duyvil?" I said in rapid frantic speculation. "But they were talking about mutual kin—nothing else." The boy said nothing. But I had sensed it instant and complete: the boy felt that, whatever of offense his mother may or may not have given, his father had given provocation; and out of the old embattled malehood, it was the hairy ineluctable Him whose guilt and shame he was going to hold preponderant. *Because now I remembered.*

"So it's Mrs. Jelliff—Sue Jelliff—and me you have got this all mixed up with," I said, figuring he must, in that fat sly nocturnal stealth that took him creeping up and down the stairs to listen when he should have been in bed, certainly have heard his mother exclaiming to his father behind that bedroom door it had been vain to close since it was not soundproof: "I saw you. I saw that with Sue. There may not be anything between you but you'd like there to be! Maybe there is at that!"

Now like a dentist forced to ruin sound enamel to reach

decayed I had to risk telling him what he did not know to keep what he assuredly did in relative control.

"This is what happened on the night in question," I said. "It was under the mistletoe, during the Holidays, at the Jelliffs'. Wait! I will be heard out! See your father as he is, but see him in no baser light. He has his arms around his neighbor's wife. It is evening, in the heat and huddled spiced felicity of the year's end, under the mistletoe (where as well as anywhere else the thirsting and exasperated flesh might be visited by the futile pangs and jets of later lust, the omnivorous aches of fifty and forty and even thirty-five to seize what may be the last of the allotted lips). Your father seems to prolong beyond its usual moment's span that custom's usufruct. Only for an instant, but in that instant letting trickle through the fissures of appearance what your mother and probably Rudy Jelliff too saw as an earnest of a flood that would have devoured that house and one four doors away."

A moon hung over the eastern roofs like a phantasmal bladder. Somewhere an icicle crashed and splintered, fruits of the day's thaw.

"So now I've got it straight," I said. "Just as through some nameless father your mother has cuckolded me (you think), so through one of Rudy Jelliff's five sons I have probably cuckolded him. Which would give you at least a half brother under that roof where under ours you have none at all. So you balance out one miscreance with another, and find your rightful kin in our poor weft of all the teeming random bonded sentient dust."

Shifting the grip, the boy walked on past the Jelliffs'.

Before him—the tracks; and beyond that—the other side of the tracks. And now out of whatever reserve capacity for astonished incredulity may yet have remained I prepared to face this last and ultimate outrage. But he didn't cross. Along our own side of the tracks ran a road which the boy turned left on. He paused before a lighted house near the corner, a white cottage with a shingle in the window which I knew from familiarity to read, "Viola Pruett, Piano Lessons," and which, like a violently unscrambled pattern on a screen, now came to focus.

Memory adumbrates just as expectation recalls. The name on the shingle made audible to listening recollection the last words of the boy's mother as she'd left, which had fallen short then of the threshold of hearing. " . . . Pruett," I remembered now. "He's going to have supper and stay with Buzzie Pruett overnight . . . Can take a few things with him in that little suitcase of his. If Mrs. Pruett phones about it, just say I'll take him over when I get back," I recalled now in that chime-counting recapitulation of retroactive memory—better than which I could not have been expected to do. Because the eternal Who-instructs might have got through to the whiskey-drinking husband or might have got through to the reader immersed in that prose vertiginous intoxicant and unique, but not to both.

"So that's it," I said. "You couldn't wait till you were taken much less till it was time but had to sneak off by yourself, and that not cross-lots but up the road I've told you a hundred times to keep off even the shoulder of."

The boy had stopped and now appeared to hesitate before

the house. He turned around at last, switched the toy and the suitcase in his hands, and started back in the direction he had come.

"What are you going back for now?" I asked.

"More stuff to take in this suitcase," he said. "I was going to just sleep at the Pruetts' overnight, but now I'm going to ask them to let me stay there for good."

—*Peter DeVries*

Just Plain Folks*

*T*he curtain has just fallen on William Faulkner's *Requiem for a Nun* (Royal Court). It has been performed with imposing devoutness by Ruth Ford, Bertice Reading, Zachary Scott and John Crawford. The production (by Tony Richardson) and the settings (by Motley) have been austerely hieratic. Let us now imagine that there steps from the wings the Stage Manager of Thornton Wilder's *Our Town*. Pulling on a corn-cob pipe, he speaks.

S. M.: "Well, folks, reckon that's about it. End of another day in the city of Jefferson, Yoknapatawpha County, Mississippi. Nothin' much happened. Couple of people got raped, couple more got their teeth kicked in, but way up there those faraway old stars are still doing their old cosmic criss-cross, and there ain't a thing we can do about it. It's pretty quiet now. Folk hereabouts get to bed early, those that can still walk. Down behind the morgue a few of the young people are roastin' a nigger over an open fire, but I guess every town has its night-owls, and afore long they'll be tucked up asleep like anybody else. Nothin' stirring down

---

* A theater review from the London *Observer* of December 1, 1957.

at the big old plantation house—you can't even hear the hummin' of that electrified barbed-wire fence, 'cause last night some drunk ran slap into it and fused the whole works. That's where Mr. Faulkner lives, and he's the fellow that thought this whole place up, kind of like God. Mr. Faulkner knows everybody round these parts like the back of his hand, 'n most everybody round these parts knows the back of Mr. Faulkner's hand. But he's not home right now, he's off on a trip round the world as Uncle Sam's culture ambassador, tellin' foreigners about how we've got to love everybody, even niggers, and how integration's bound to happen in a few thousand years anyway, so we might just as well make haste slowly. Ain't a thing we can do about it.

(He takes out his watch and consults it.)

Along about now the good folk of Jefferson City usually get around to screamin' in their sleep. Just ordinary people havin' ordinary nightmares, the way most of us do most of the time.

(An agonized shrieking is briefly heard.)

Ayeah, there they go. Nothin' wrong there that an overdose of Seconal won't fix.

(He pockets his watch.)

Like I say, simple folk fussin' and botherin' over simple, eternal problems. Take this Temple Stevens, the one Mr. Faulkner's been soundin' off about. 'Course, Mr. Faulkner don't pretend to be a real play-writer, 'n maybe that's why he tells the whole story backwards, 'n why he takes up so much time gabbin' about people you never met—and what's more, ain't going to meet. By the time he's told you what happened before you got here, it's gettin' to be time to go home. But we were talkin' about Temple. Ain't nothin' special about her. Got herself mixed up in an auto accident—witnessed a killin'—got herself locked up in a sportin' house with one of these seck-sual perverts—witnessed another killin'—got herself married up 'n bore a couple of fine kids. Then, just's she's fixing to run off with a blackmailer, her maid Nancy—that's the nigger dope-fiend she met in the cathouse—takes a notion to murder her baby boy. That's all about Temple—just a run of bad luck that could happen to anyone. And don't come askin' me why Nancy murders the kid. Accordin' to Mr. Faulkner, she does it to keep him from bein' tainted by his mother's sins. Seems to me even an ignorant nigger would know a tainted child was better'n a dead one, but I guess I can't get under their skins the way Mr. Faulkner can.

(He glances up at the sky.)

Movin' along towards dawn in our town. Pretty soon folks'll start up on that old diurnal round of sufferin' and expiatin' and spoutin' sentences two pages long. One way or another, an awful lot of sufferin' gets done around here. 'Specially by the black folk—'n that's how it should be, 'cause they don't feel it like we do, 'n anyways, they've got that simple primitive faith to lean back on.

(He consults his watch again.)

Well, Temple's back with her husband, and in a couple of minutes they'll be hangin' Nancy. Maybe that's why darkies were born—to keep white marriages from bustin' up. Anyways, a lot of things have happened since the curtain went up to-night. Six billion gallons of water have tumbled over Niagara Falls. Three thousand boys and girls took their first puff of marijuana, 'n a puppy-dog in a flyin' coffin was sighted over Alaska. Most of you out there've been admirin' Miss Ruth Ford's play-actin', 'n a few of you've been won-derin' whether she left her pay-thos in the dressing-room or whether maybe she didn't have any to begin with. Out in Hollywood a big producer's been readin' Mr. Faulkner's book and figurin' whether to buy the movie rights for Miss Joan Crawford. Right enough, all over the world, it's been quite an evening. 'N now Nancy's due for the drop.

(*A thud offstage. The Stage Manager smiles philosophically.*) Ayeah, that's it—right on time.

(*He re-pockets his watch.*) That's the end of the play, friends. You can go out and push dope now, those of you that push dope. Down in our town there's a meetin' of the Deathwish Committee, 'n a fund-raisin' rally in aid of Holocaust Relief, 'n all over town the prettiest gals're primping themselves up for the big beauty prize—Miss Cegenation of 1957. There's always somethin' happenin'. Why—over at the schoolhouse an old-fashioned-type humanist just shot himself. *You* get a good rest, too. Good-night."

(*He exits. A sound of Bibles being thumped momentarily fills the air.*)

—*Kenneth Tynan*

Go Down, Faulkner
(In the Throes of William Faulkner's
Go Down, Moses)

●　●　●　●　●　*S*artoris Tsouris, oldest daughter of Commander Sutpen who was expelled from school in his twelfth year because of insubordination, mother of half a county and grandmother of a neighboring town, older than God and as popular.

They were bringing in his body past the white gate, through the white palings old now and broken in spots, and perhaps even a little disheveled, and the Cunnel said "Here they come," and Buck and Bubbles watching it go by, into the garden and through the radishes and up past the front steps and into Uncle Buck's room where he, roused from sleep, stirring and stretching, was crying out "Get that goddam fox out of here, you damn fox," and then up behind the clock. Uncle Buck had never owned a necktie; when he were with the Sartoris bodies, to visit the neighbors, or to bring back Tomey's Turl, Uncle Bubbles went.

Old Ike snorted. "Fine piece o' horseflesh," he said, remembering the battles and the horses down, Gettysburg and the charges. "Eggs," he said. "The man says he sits on eggs."

And Bill Faulkner, watching Uncle Buck and Uncle

Bubbles, feeling the horse's strong leg pressing on his, "Got a jug here says it's one damn hell horse. Got a brother John swear to anything I say."

And old Sartoris Tsouris sitting on the front stoop rocking and sitting, thinking perhaps of Buck and Bubbles and perhaps only of the fox, remembering perhaps the old days and the Sutpen boys and the white palings new and not broken, remembering the old Sartoris and Tomey's Turl when old Ike McCaslin and Major Faulkner shook dice in the long afternoon, sitting in the shade of the magnolias shaking dice in the long afternoon in the shade of the magnolias.

"I'll shake you for your daughter and six niggers," old Ike had said, grandfather of ten counties and brother to six.

"Against what, you old hellion?" Major Faulkner had said, thinking of the plate glass window and his daughter rocking on the front stoop, and the horse and his daughter down in the field and the sudden quick escape of the fox.

"Against the three hundred Confederate dollars you owe for that horse," old McIke cackled cannily, possibly brother to seven.

"Old John Sartoris Faulkner? Four counties away?" Uncle Buck pulled nervously at his necktie. Young John it was, he remembered, sloppy breeches and all, and old Sartoris Tsouris, coming out of the magnolias shamefaced and Uncle Buck waiting by the white gate, "What have you done, you fool?" Pulling young John aside and thinking of Tomey's Turl, "What have you done, you young fool? Sartoris Tsouris and half the county."

And the fox, now on top of the clock and looking down

like a bright-eyed Tomey's Turl, looking like another Sartoris, perhaps, with its bright eyes and rotten flesh, possibly
itself remembering the rain and the front stoop and dogs,
all in a row and panting, and the horse down and old Sartoris
Tsouris crying noisily into the magnolias.

Tomey's Turl, faced with a white man and quivering,
seeing the pistol, said: "Ah wants a jug."

"A jug?" said the white man, "You mean a pint." He
pointed the pistol at old McIke. "This here's Friday."

"Tsah!" said old McIke, looking at Tomey's Turl, one
day to be father to the Sutpens, to old Sartoris Tsouris, out
in the field, to a new county. Old Ike took a pull from the
jug. "Fine piece o' jug," he said.

"Damn nigger's run off again," Uncle Buck said, putting
on his necktie. "Damn fox."

"I never say a thing," Bill Faulkner said to the horse, its
strong leg against his, its long length on the ground, eyes
so much like the fox's, like Ike McCaslin's gleaming past
the jug, the eggs scattered and broken, and young John
trying to speak. "I never say a thing about this horse but
that brother John, you know him you say, brother John will
back me up. Maybe he sits on eggs, I don't know, maybe
he doesn't, but brother John will back me up."

"Damn nigger's off again," Uncle Bubbles said. "Damn
hell fox."

"There was a little Tomey," said Uncle Buck, "and she
had a little Turl right in the middle of her forehead."

He wants it that way, he was thinking, *that's the way he
always wanted it, right like that, with flowers and a casket and
lying in the field with her and coming through the white fence*

slowly, past the broken palings. With flowers, and with a casket.
He always wanted it that way, and what he wanted he always
got.

"I remember old Sartoris Faulkner," Ike McCaslin said, putting down the jug, "always out in the bushes with someone. Tomey's Turl, most likely, although sometimes one of the Sutpen girls."

"Perhaps he sits on fish, too," old Bill Faulkner said dreamily, "Brother John will swear to it if I say so."

Ike McCaslin grinned. "And when Bill was bad," he said, yawning noisily, "he was horrid."

—Shirley Jackson

From *Sylvester the Cat*

• • • • • *A*nd get the hell on outa this kitchen! came
with the hard rush of the maid's brush and a door banged
and light from the kitchen got swept quick off the dusty
yard and the two of them, the one tall and supple and black
as molasses blacker than the night that held them there in
its soft palpable grip blacker even than negroes, lisped with
an almost feline intensity a curse incomprehensible and fleet
and waved white palms in anguished yet unvanquished
frenzy so that the other, the smaller longsuffering foil to
and recipient of vicious and obsessional cruelty at last saw
that a chance to alter the theme of their inexplicable and
prime-time-honored bondage from one of antagonism to
one of complicity might be to say *They all so crazy in this
country that you and me Sylvester we better team up fer pertection*
so that *Yeth thir!* the first might say, long tongue fleering
on the lips of his mouth *We gotta think of thom way of getting
uth thom boidtheed, sshlurrp.*

—*Derek Willey*

Afternoon of a Cow

. . . . . . Mr. Faulkner and I were sitting under the mulberry with the afternoon's first julep while he informed me what to write on the morrow, when Oliver appeared suddenly around the corner of the smokehouse, running and with his eyes looking quite large and white. "Mr. Bill!" he cried. "Day done sot fire to de pasture!"

"———" cried Mr. Faulkner, with that promptitude which quite often marks his actions, "——— those boys to ———!" springing up and referring to his own son, Malcolm, and to his brother's son, James, and to the cook's son, Rover or Grover. Grover his name is, though both Malcolm and James (they and Grover are of an age and have, indeed, grown up not only contemporaneously but almost inextricably) have insisted upon calling him Rover since they could speak, so that now all the household, including the child's own mother and naturally the child itself, call him Rover too, with the exception of myself, whose practice and belief it has never been to call any creature, man, woman, child or beast, out of its rightful name—just as I permit no one to call me out of mine, though I am aware that behind my back both Malcolm and James (and doubtless Rover or Grover) refer to me as Ernest be Toogood—a crass and low form of so-called wit or humor to which children, these two in particular—are only too prone. I have attempted on more than one occasion (this was years ago; I have long since ceased) to explain to them that my position in the household is in no sense menial, since I have been writing Mr. Faulkner's novels and short stories for years. But I long ago became convinced (and even reconciled) that neither of them either knew or cared about the meaning of the term.

I do not think that I anticipate myself in saying that we did not know where the three boys would now be. We would not be expected to know, beyond a general feeling or conviction that they would by now be concealed in the loft of the barn or stable—this from previous experience, though experience had never before included or comprised arson. Nor do I feel that I further violate the formal rules of order, unity and emphasis by saying that we would never for one moment have conceived them to be where later evidence indicated that they now were. But more on this subject anon: we were not thinking of the boys now; as Mr. Faulkner himself might have observed, someone should have been thinking about them ten or fifteen minutes ago; that now it was too late. No, our concern was to reach the pasture, though not with any hope of saving the hay which had been Mr. Faulkner's pride and even hope—a fine, though small, plantation of this grain or forage fenced lightly away from the pasture proper and the certain inroads of the three stocks whose pleasance the pasture was, which had been intended as an alternative or balancing factor in

the winter's victualing of the three beasts. We had no hope
of saving this, since the month was September following a
dry summer, and we knew that this as well as the remainder
of the pasture would burn with almost the instantaneous
celerity of gunpowder or celluloid. That is, I had no hope
of it and doubtless Oliver had no hope of it. I do not know
what Mr. Faulkner's emotion was, since it appears (or so I
have read and heard) a fundamental human trait to decline
to recognize misfortune with regard to some object which
man either desires or already possesses and holds dear, until
it has run him down and then over like a Juggernaut itself.
I do not know if this emotion would function in the presence
of a field of hay, since I have neither owned nor desired to
own one. No, it was not the hay which we were concerned
about. It was the three animals, the two horses and the cow,
in particular the cow, who, less gifted or equipped for speed
than the horses, might be overtaken by the flames and
perhaps asphyxiated, or at least so badly scorched as to be
rendered temporarily unfit for her natural function; and that
the two horses might bolt in terror, and to their detriment,
into the further fence of barbed wire or might even turn
and rush back into the actual flames, as is one of the more
intelligent characteristics of this so-called servant and friend
of man.

So, led by Mr. Faulkner and not even waiting to go
around to the arched passage, we burst through the hedge
itself and, led by Mr. Faulkner who moved at a really as-
tonishing pace for a man of what might be called almost
violently sedentary habit by nature, we ran across the yard
and through Mrs. Faulkner's flower beds and then through

her rose garden, although I will say that both Oliver and myself made some effort to avoid the plants; and on across the adjacent vegetable garden, where even Mr. Faulkner could accomplish no harm since at this season of the year it was innocent of edible matter; and on to the panel pasture fence over which Mr. Faulkner hurled himself with that same agility and speed and palpable disregard of limb which was actually amazing—not only because of his natural lethargic humor, which I have already indicated, but because of that shape and figure which ordinarily accompanies it (or at least does so in Mr. Faulkner's case)—and were enveloped immediately in smoke.

But it was at once evident by its odor that this came, not from the hay which must have stood intact even if not green and then vanished in holocaust doubtless during the few seconds while Oliver was crying his news, but, from the cedar grove at the pasture's foot. Nevertheless, odor or not, its pall covered the entire visible scene, although ahead of us we could see the creeping line of conflagration beyond which the three unfortunate beasts now huddled or rushed in terror of their lives. Or so we thought until, still led by Mr. Faulkner and hastening now across a stygian and desolate floor which almost at once became quite unpleasant to the soles of the feet and promised to become more so, something monstrous and wild of shape rushed out of the smoke. It was the larger horse, Stonewall—a congenitally vicious brute which no one durst approach save Mr. Faulkner and Oliver, and not even Oliver durst mount (though why either Oliver or Mr. Faulkner should want to is forever beyond me) which rushed down upon us with the evident intent of taking advantage of this opportunity to destroy its owner and attendant both, with myself included for lagniappe or perhaps for pure hatred of the entire human race. It evidently altered its mind, however, swerving and vanishing again into smoke. Mr. Faulkner and Oliver had paused and given it but a glance. "I reckin dey all right," Oliver said. "But where you reckin Beulah at?"

"On the other side of that ———— fire, backing up in front of it and bellowing," replied Mr. Faulkner. He was correct, because almost at once we began to hear the poor creature's lugubrious lamenting. I have often remarked now how both Mr. Faulkner and Oliver apparently possess some curious rapport with horned and hooved beasts and even dogs, which I cheerfully admit that I do not possess myself and do not even understand. That is, I cannot understand it in Mr. Faulkner. With Oliver, of course, cattle of all kinds might be said to be his avocation, and his dallying (that is the exact word; I have watched him more than once, motionless and apparently pensive and really almost pilgrimlike, with the handle of the mower or hoe or rake for support) with lawn mower and gardening tools his sideline or hobby. But Mr. Faulkner, a member in good standing of the ancient and gentle profession of letters! But then neither can I understand why he should wish to ride a horse, and the notion has occurred to me that Mr. Faulkner acquired his rapport gradually and perhaps over a long period of time from contact of his posterior with the animal he bestrode.

We hastened on toward the sound of the doomed creature's bellowing. I thought that it came from the flames

perhaps and was the final plaint of her agony—a dumb
brute's indictment of heaven itself—but Oliver said not,
that it came from beyond the fire. Now there occurred in
it a most peculiar alteration. It was not an increase in terror,
which scarcely could have been possible. I can describe it
best by saying that she now sounded as if she had descended
abruptly into the earth. This we found to be true. I believe
however that this time order requires, and the element of
suspense and surprise which the Greeks themselves have
authorized will permit, that the story progress in the se-
quence of events as they occurred to the narrator, even
though the accomplishment of the actual event recalled to
the narrator the fact or circumstance with which he was
already familiar and of which the reader should have been
previously made acquainted. So I shall proceed.

Imagine us, then, hastening (even if the abysmal terror
in the voice of the hapless beast had not been inventive
enough, we had another: on the morrow, when I raised one
of the shoes which I had worn on this momentous afternoon,
the entire sole crumbled into a substance resembling nothing
so much as that which might have been scraped from the
ink-wells of childhood's school days at the beginning of the
fall term) across that stygian plain, our eyes and lungs
smarting with that smoke along whose further edge the
border of fire crept. Again a wild and monstrous shape
materialized in violent motion before us, again apparently
with the avowed and frantic aim of running us down. For
a horrid moment I believed it to be the horse, Stonewall,
returned because after passing us for some distance (persons
do this; possibly it might likewise occur in an animal, its

finer native senses dulled with smoke and terror), remembering having seen myself or recognized me, and had now returned to destroy me alone. I had never liked the horse. It was an emotion even stronger than mere fear; it was that horrified disgust which I imagine one must feel toward a python and doubtless even the horse's subhuman sensibilities had felt and had come to reciprocate. I was mistaken, however. It was the other horse, the smaller one which Malcolm and James rode, apparently with enjoyment, as though in miniature of the besotted perversion of their father and uncle—an indiscriminate, round-bodied creature, as gentle as the larger one was vicious, with a drooping sad upper lip and an inarticulate and bemused (though to me still sly and untrustworthy) gaze; it, too, swerved past us and also vanished just before we reached the line of flame which was neither as large nor as fearful as it had looked, though the smoke was thicker, and seemed to be filled with the now loud terrified voice of the cow. In fact, the poor creature's voice seemed now to be everywhere: in the air above us and in the earth beneath. With Mr. Faulkner still in the lead we sprang over it, whereupon Mr. Faulkner immediately vanished. Still in the act of running, he simply vanished out of the smoke before the eyes of Oliver and myself as though he too had dropped into the earth.

This is what he had also done. With the voice of Mr. Faulkner and the loud terror of the cow coming out of the earth at our feet and the creeping line of the conflagration just behind us, I now realized what had happened and so solved Mr. Faulkner's disappearance as well as the previous alteration in the voice of the cow. I now realized that, confused by the smoke and the incandescent sensation about the soles of the feet, I had become disoriented and had failed to be aware that all the while we had been approaching a gully or ravine of whose presence I was quite aware, having looked down into it more than once while strolling in the afternoons while Mr. Faulkner would be riding the large horse, and upon whose brink or verge Oliver and I now stood and into which Mr. Faulkner and the cow had, in turn and in the reverse order, fallen.

"Are you hurt, Mr. Faulkner?" I cried. I shall not attempt to reproduce Mr. Faulkner's reply, other than to indicate that it was couched in that pure ancient classic Saxon which the best of our literature sanctions and authorizes and which, due to the exigencies of Mr. Faulkner's style and subject matter, I often employ but which I myself never use although Mr. Faulkner even in his private life is quite addicted to it and which, when he employs it, indicates what might be called a state of the most robust, even though not at all calm, wellbeing. So I knew that he was not hurt. "What shall we now do?" I inquired of Oliver.

"We better git down in dat hole too," Oliver replied. "Ain't you feel dat fire right behime us?" I had forgot about the fire in my concern over Mr. Faulkner, but upon glancing behind me I felt instinctively that Oliver was right. So we scrambled or fell down the steep sandy declivity, to the bottom of the ravine where Mr. Faulkner, still speaking, stood and where the cow was now safely ensconced though still in a state of complete hysteria, from which point or sanctuary we watched the conflagration pass over, the flames crumbling and flickering and dying away along the brink of the ravine. Then Mr. Faulkner spoke:

"Go catch Dan, and bring the big rope from the storehouse."

"Do you mean me?" said I. Mr. Faulkner did not reply, so he and I stood beside the cow who did not yet seem to realize that the danger was past or perhaps whose more occult brute intellect knew that the actual suffering and outrage and despair had yet to occur—and watched Oliver climb or scramble back up the declivity. He was gone for some time, although after a while he returned, leading the smaller and tractable horse who was adorned with a section of harness, and carrying the rope; whereupon commenced the arduous business of extricating the cow. One end of the rope was attached to her horns, she still objecting violently; the other end was attached to the horse. "What shall I do?" I inquired.

"Push," said Mr. Faulkner.

"Where shall I push?" I asked.

"I don't give a ———," said Mr. Faulkner. "Just push."

But it appeared that it could not be done. The creature resisted, perhaps to the pull of the rope or perhaps to Oliver's encouraging shouts and cries from the brink overhead or possibly to the motive power supplied by Mr. Faulkner (he was directly behind, almost beneath her, his shoulder against her buttocks or loins and swearing steadily now) and myself. She made a gallant effort, scrambled quite half way up the declivity, lost her footing and slid back. Once more we tried and failed, and then again. And then a most regrettable accident occurred. This third time the rope either slipped or parted, and Mr. Faulkner and the cow were hurled violently to the foot of the precipice with Mr. Faulkner underneath.

Later—that evening, to be exact—I recalled how, at the moment while we watched Oliver scramble out of the ravine, I seem to have received, as though by telepathy, from the poor creature (a female mind; the lone female among three men) not only her terror but the subject of it: that she knew by woman's sacred instinct that the future held for her that which is to a female far worse than any fear of bodily injury or suffering: one of those invasions of female privacy where, helpless victim of her own physical body, she seems to see herself as object of some malignant power for irony and outrage; and this none the less bitter for the fact that those who are to witness it, gentlemen though they be, will never be able to forget it but will walk the earth with the remembrance of it so long as she lives;—yes, even the more bitter for the fact that they who are to witness it are gentlemen, people of her own class. Remember how the poor spent terrified creature had for an entire afternoon been the anguished and blind victim of a circumstance which it could not comprehend, had been sported with by an element which it instinctively feared, and had now been hurled recently and violently down a precipice whose crest it doubtless now believed it would never see again.—I have been told by soldiers (I served in France, in the Y.M.C.A.) how, upon entering battle, there often sets up within them, prematurely as it were, a certain impulse or desire which brings on a result quite logical and quite natural, the fulfillment of which is incontestable and of course irrevocable.—In a word, Mr. Faulkner underneath received the full discharge of the poor creature's afternoon of anguish and despair.

It has been my fortune or misfortune to lead what is—
or might be—called a quiet, even though not retired, life;
and I have even preferred to acquire my experience from
reading what had happened to others or what other men
believe or think might have logically happened to creatures
of their invention or even in inventing what Mr. Faulkner
conceives might have happened to certain and sundry creatures who compose his novels and stories. Nevertheless, I
would imagine that a man is never too old nor too secure
to suffer what might be called experiences of initial and
bizarre originality, though of course not always outrage,
following which his reaction would be quite almost invari-
ably out of character. Or rather, following which his reaction
would reveal that actual character which for years he may
have successfully concealed from the public, his intimates,
and his wife and family; perhaps even from himself. I would
take it to be one of these which Mr. Faulkner had just
suffered.

Anyway, his actions during the subsequent few minutes
were most peculiar for him. The cow—poor female alone
among three men—struggled up almost at once and stood,
hysterically still though no longer violent, trembling rather
with a kind of aghast abasement not yet become despair.
But for a time Mr. Faulkner, prone on the earth, did not
stir at all. Then he rose. He said, "Wait," which naturally
we should do until he gave further orders or instructions.
Then—the poor cow and myself, and Oliver looking down
from the crest beside the horse—we watched Mr. Faulkner
walk quietly a few paces down the ravine and sit down, his
elbows on his knees and his chin supported between his

hands. It was not the sitting down which was peculiar. Mr. Faulkner did this often—steadily perhaps is a better word—if not in the house, then (in summer) well down in a large chair on the veranda just outside the library window where I would be working, his feet on the railing, reading a detective magazine; in winter in the kitchen, his stocking feet inside the oven to the stove. It was the attitude in which he now sat. As I have indicated, there was a quality almost violent about Mr. Faulkner's sedentation; it would be immobile without at all being lethargic, if I may put it so. He now sat in the attitude of M. Rodin's *Penseur* increased to his tenth geometric power say, since *le penseur's* principal bewilderment appears to be at what has bemused him, while Mr. Faulkner can have had no doubt. We watched him quietly—myself, and the poor cow who now stood with her head lowered and not even trembling in utter and now hopeless female shame; Oliver and the horse on the brink above. I remarked then that Oliver no longer had smoke for his background. The immediate conflagration was now over, though the cedar grove would doubtless smolder until the equinox.

Then Mr. Faulkner rose. He returned quietly and he spoke as quietly (or even more so) to Oliver as I have ever heard him: "Drop the rope, Jack." Oliver removed his end of the rope from the horse and dropped it, and Mr. Faulkner took it up and turned and led the cow down the ravine. For a moment I watched him with an amazement of which Oliver doubtless partook; in the next moment doubtless Oliver and I would have looked at one another in that same astonishment. But we did not; we moved; doubtless we moved at the same moment. Oliver did not even bother to descend into the ravine. He just went around it while I hastened on and overtook Mr. Faulkner and the cow; indeed, the three of us were actually soldiers recovered from the amnesia of battle, the battle with the flames for the life of the cow. It has been often remarked and even insisted upon in literature (novels have been built upon it, though none of them are Mr. Faulkner's) how, when faced with catastrophe, man does everything but the simple one. But from the fund of my own experience, though it does consist almost entirely of that afternoon, it is my belief that it is in the face of danger and disaster that he does the simple thing. It is merely simply wrong.

We moved down the ravine to where it turned at right angles and entered the woods which descended to its level. With Mr. Faulkner and the cow in the lead we turned up through the woods and came presently to the black desolation of the pasture in the fence to which Oliver, waiting, had already contrived a gap or orifice through which we passed. Then with Mr. Faulkner again in the lead and with Oliver, leading the horse and the cow, and myself side by side, we retraced across that desolate plain the course of our recent desperate race to offer succor, though bearing somewhat to the left in order to approach the stable—or barnlot. We had almost reached the late hay plantation when, without warning, we found ourselves faced by three apparitions. They were not ten paces away when we saw them and I believe that neither Mr. Faulkner nor Oliver recognized them at all, though I did. In fact, I had an instantaneous and curious sense, not that I had anticipated this moment so much as that I had been waiting for it over a period which might be computed in years.

Imagine yourself, if you will, set suddenly down in a world in complete ocular or chromatic reversal. Imagine yourself faced with three small ghosts, not of white but of purest and unrelieved black. The mind, the intelligence, simply refuses to believe that they should have taken refuge from their recent crime or misdemeanor in the hay plantation before it took fire, and lived. Yet there they were. Apparently they had neither brows, lashes nor hair; and clothing epidermis and all, they were of one identical sable, and the only way in which Rover or Grover could be distinguished from the other two was by Malcolm's and James' blue eyes. They stood looking at us in complete immobility until Mr. Faulkner said, again with that chastened gentleness and quietude which, granted my theory that the soul, plunged without warning into some unforeseen and outrageous catastrophe, comes out in its true colors, has been Mr. Faulkner's true and hidden character all these years: "Go to the house."

They turned and vanished immediately, since it had been only by the eyeballs that we had distinguished them from the stygian surface of the earth at all. They may have preceded us or we may have passed them. I do not know. At least, we did not see them again, because presently we quitted the sable plain which had witnessed our Gethsemane, and presently entered the barnlot where Mr. Faulkner turned and took the halter of the horse while Oliver led the cow into its private and detached domicile, from which there came presently the sound of chewing as, freed now of anguish and shame she ruminated, maiden meditant and—I hope—once more fancy free.

Mr. Faulkner stood in the door of the stable (within which, by and by, I could hear the larger and vicious horse, Stonewall, already at his food, stamp now and then or strike the board wall with his hoof as though even in the act of eating it could not forbear making sounds of threat and derision toward the very man whose food nourished it) and removed his clothing. Then, in full sight of the house and of whoever might care or not care to see, he lathered himself with saddle soap and then stood at the watering trough while Oliver doused or flushed him down with pail after pail of water. "Never mind the clothes just now," he said to Oliver. "Get me a drink."

"Make it two," said I; I felt that the occasion justified, even though it may not have warranted, that temporary aberration into the vernacular of the fleeting moment. So presently, Mr. Faulkner now wearing a light summer horse blanket belonging to Stonewall, we sat again beneath the mulberry with the second julep of the afternoon.

"Well, Mr. Faulkner," said I after a time, "shall we continue?"

"Continue what?" said Mr. Faulkner.

"Your suggestions for tomorrow," said I. Mr. Faulkner said nothing at all. He just drank, with that static violence which was his familiar character, and so I knew that he was himself once more and that the real Mr. Faulkner which had appeared momentarily to Oliver and myself in the pasture had already retreated to that inaccessible bourn from which only the cow, Beulah, had ever evoked it, and that doubtless we would never see it again. So after a time I said, "Then, with your permission, tomorrow I shall venture into fact and employ the material which we ourselves have this afternoon created."

"Do so," Mr. Faulkner said—shortly, I thought.

"Only," I continued, "I shall insist upon my prerogative and right to tell this one in my own diction and style, and not yours."

"By ———!" said Mr. Faulkner. "You better had."

—Ernest V. Trueblood
(William Faulkner)

Grateful acknowledgment is given for permission to reprint the following material:

"Requiem for a Noun, or Intruder in the Dusk" from *Without a Stitch in Time,* by Peter DeVries. Copyright 1950 by Peter DeVries. First appeared in *The New Yorker.* Reprinted with permission of Little, Brown and Company and Watkins/Loomis Agency, Inc.

"Just Plain Folks," by Kenneth Tynan, originally published in the London *Observer* dated 1 December 1957. Reprinted with permission of Kathleen Tynan.

"Go Down, Faulkner (In the Throes of William Faulkner's *Go Down, Moses*)," by Shirley Jackson, from the Library of Congress manuscript division. Reprinted with permission of the Estate of Shirley Jackson.

"From *Sylvester the Cat,*" by Derek Willey, originally published in the *New Statesman* dated 15 February 1974. Reprinted with permission of the *Observer.*

"Afternoon of a Cow," by Ernest V. Trueblood (William Faulkner), from the *Uncollected Stories of William Faulkner.* Reprinted with permission of Random House, Inc.

Illustrations by Tullio Pericoli, Edward Sorel,
Covarrubias, Rick Geary, Gerry Gersten, David Levine,
Richard Thompson, and David Levine appear on
pages 2, 12, 38, 62, 84, 100, 114, and 134, respectively.
The publisher is grateful to the L. D. Brodsky Collection
for providing the illustration found on page 38.